To my husband Philip:
The source of all those good genes
and
To our children, Gordon, Peter, Paula, and Neva:
who express them so well

Fast and Delicious

Cookbook

by Rose Grant

illustrated by Dorothy Cutright Davis

ISBN 0-911954-62-7
Library of Congress Catalog Card Number: 81-81484

TABLE OF CONTENTS

INTRODUCTION

Let me share a cook's fantasy:

It begins with a beautifully equipped kitchen, six uninterrupted hours to create a meal, all exotic ingredients at hand. An aide miraculously appears when a counter has to be cleared or some mundane task performed. Of course, in this fantasy money and calories don't count.

Reality is quite another matter:

The kitchen is small, with limited counter space. There is no aide. Shopping is often done on the way home from work at the most convenient supermarket. An hour or so is usually the maximum time that can be given to the preparation of a meal; you're too tired for any elaborate procedures. And of course, money and calories do count.

Fast and Delicious has been written for busy people, for working people. Though they want to eat well, they are involved in many other things and have limited time and energy to devote to meal preparation.

Often the directions given for a recipe seem too complicated and time consuming to tackle at the end of a working day. The trick is to take shortcuts without compromising quality. It is possible to simplify many procedures, even cut out a few, and still come up with a delicious dish.

Fast and Delicious incorporates the shortcuts into the recipes. The emphasis is on fewer ingredients; nothing has to be stirred constantly or watched. The number of bowls and utensils is also kept to a minimum, since clean-up is part of meal preparation. Everything is done with an eye on the clock.

Good cooking starts with a respectful attitude toward food. If we think of vegetables as having worked hard to become food on our plates, we owe them the courtesy of not cooking them beyond recognition. No fish should die to become a fishstick. Any chicken deserves a better fate than to wind up as a TV dinner. If you have ever tasted a roast beef that spent several hours on a steam table and thought "a cow died for this?" you're on the right track. We cannot help but turn out better meals if we appreciate food, and good cookbooks encourage this appreciation.

The cookbook you reach for again and again must somehow anticipate your mood and your time limitations, the leftovers in the refrigerator that need eating, and how much of your shopping list you will remember without having remembered to take the shopping list. The recipes that you use all the time must not only be easy to follow, they must also be adaptable, meaning that as long as you follow the basic recipe, you can omit, double, or substitute many ingredients without disastrous results. You will soon find, as most cooks do, that some of your best creations are the recipes you just "throw together."

If the recipe calls for breadcrumbs and you don't have any, but do have some wilting potato chips, you can put the chips in the oven for a few minutes, crush them, and use them in place of the breadcrumbs. In addition to feeling virtuous at having rescued the potato chips, you will have invented your own recipe, which is probably much better than the original. What is most important—you are developing the right attitude toward "The Recipe." You see it as a road map, nothing more.

The recipes in *Fast and Delicious* have been collected and adapted over the past 25 years. They have evolved to keep up with our changing ideas about what constitutes good eating. We now know that it is not necessary (or even desirable) to cook with a pitcher of heavy cream in one hand and a pound of butter in the other. Eating meat twice a day is no longer considered the best source of protein. There is increasing acceptance of vegetables and grains in our diet, which add variety, as well as nutrition. There are times when you want to go all out on a fantastic entree or dessert, when money and calories really don't count. But, for the meals you eat every day, fewer processed foods, less sugar and salt, and fewer calories is a more healthy and intelligent approach to the problem of "What shall we eat?" And the solution can be found in *Fast and Delicious*.

The Kitchen

Fast and delicious meals can be created with very simple equipment. Even though fine kitchen tools are not essential, when time counts, the value of a few obedient, dependable servants, that do what they are supposed to do—the first time—cannot be overstated.

Quality knives that cut without sawing, kitchen scissors that can cut through a chicken bone without leaving a permanent dent in your thumb, a "smart" food processor that forgives you even when you put too much into it, are a pleasure to use because they simplify mundane chores. A cook who turns out fast and delicious meals deserves heavy well-balanced pots and pans that don't fight with you. Fine quality cookware sits squarely on the stove and is much easier to clean. Food doesn't burn as readily in it as it does in flimsy cookware.

Any tool you buy for the kitchen is a long-term investment and should be of good quality. Multi-purpose gadgets usually serve no purpose well. What's more, they don't even have the decency to get lost or broken. They just hang around and take up space. Almost every kitchen has a drawer full of old gadgets that should be thrown out, their original purpose long forgotten.

Just as you can create fast and delicious meals with simple equipment, you can also do it with ingredients found in any supermarket. However, as you cook more, your standards go up and your palate improves. Though there is nothing wrong with using ordinary salad oil in Italian spaghetti sauce, olive oil has a more "authentic" taste. You may have gotten along happily for years with the grated Parmesan cheese found on the shelf in the supermarket. But, once you have tasted the imported kind that you grate yourself, you may find you prefer it.

A fast and delicious cook should keep a stock of essential foods in the pantry ready for use. A jar of marinated artichoke hearts, a can of minced clams and three tablespoons of imported Parmesan cheese can hide the fact that you ran out of time and had to start with canned spaghetti sauce. The essentials will vary from cook to cook, but there is a wonderful feeling of security knowing that you have a well stocked pantry. In cooking, nothing is carved in stone. Though it is a good idea to stock your pantry with fine ingredients, substitutions are always possible. If you misplace the pepper grinder, the meal will not be ruined. Though it gives you the feeling that you are doing something special to use freshly ground pepper, I doubt many people have palates so refined that they can tell the difference between freshly ground pepper and the pepper shaken from a tin.

The following is a list of MY essentials. Many of these items are used in this cookbook.

FRESH: garlic, shallots, dill, chives, parsley, ginger root, lemons, limes, mushrooms, horseradish, plain yogurt, mayonnaise, sour cream, cream cheese, imported Parmesan, Romano, Cheddar, Gruyere, Bleu cheese

FROZEN: chives, chopped onion, spinach

DRIED: oregano, basil, curry, marjoram, dill, tarragon, paprika, rosemary, garlic and onion powder, thyme, sage, cayenne pepper, mustard, peppercorns, dehydrated onion, lemon pepper, ginger, cinnamon, nutmeg, cloves

PANTRY SHELF: bouillon cubes, canned chicken broth, canned beef broth, dried onion soup, cream of mushroom soup (and a few others) for sauces, canned Italian tomatoes, tomato sauce, tomato paste, dried spaghetti sauce mix, canned spaghetti sauce, canned tuna and salmon, Chinese rice vinegar, wine vinegar, olive oil, peanut oil, imported soy sauce, Worchestershire sauce, Tabasco, sauce, Dijon mustard, reconstituted lemon juice, marinated artichoke hearts, capers, anchovy filets, chopped pimento, chopped ripe olives, green olives, water chestnuts, breadcrumbs, skimmed milk powder, assorted chopped nuts, raisins, graham cracker crumbs, baking soda and baking powder, biscuit mix, cornstarch, cake mixes

WINES: dry sherry, Madeira, rum, chablis (dry white wine), burgundy (dry red wine)

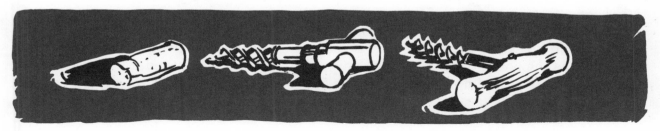

Biography

Although I majored in psychology at Hunter College in New York, I never pursued a career. I married soon after graduation and 4 children followed in fairly rapid succession. My occupation for many years has been wife and mother.

We moved frequently in the early years of our marriage to New York, Philadelphia, Baltimore and Washington, following the trail of my husband's career as a biologist.

No matter where we were, I found time for my hobby of collecting recipes and trying them out on my family. Our family dinner each evening was the most important event of the day and I tried to make the meals special. But with the demands of 4 children I never seemed to have enough time to do it right. I was constantly looking for meals that were fast and delicious. As my recipe collection increased, I became pretty good at it. I found short cuts that didn't change the recipe but did knock out several steps in its preparation. I soon became a source of fast and delicious recipes for friends and neighbors.

When my children began to leave the nest, I decided to take on a career. I returned to school and got a Master of Library Science degree at the University of Oregon; my husband was then on the faculty of the University. When I graduated, I became a school librarian. It was more important than ever to find fast and delicious meals. After a day of coping with second graders looking for books on dinosaurs, I didn't have the energy or the inclination to do anything more.

But after a while I had had enough of teaching. In recent years I have turned my hobby into a vocation, which I combined with my library skills. I am now a book indexer; cookbooks, of course, are my specialty. But more exciting than that, I have devised a recipe retrieval system which gives any recipe collector instant access to all the recipes in his/her collection. I am in the process of marketing my invention.

Fast and Delicious is my first cookbook. I have enough recipes in my retrieval system for Fast and Delicious II and possibly Fast and Delicious III.

Our permanent home is in Eugene, Oregon, but our spiritual home and our closest ties are in Woods Hole, Massachusetts, where we happily spend our summers.

APPETIZERS

Appetizers are the promise of things to come. Ideally, they should set the tone of the meal. But, when we are pushed for time, appetizers are often an afterthought. The same ones are served again and again: store-bought dip and chips, a piece of cheese and some crackers or peanuts in a dish.

The recipes in this section have been selected for ease of preparation and for eye appeal. Though each takes just a few minutes to prepare, all of them can be prepared ahead. All of these appetizers are intended to go with drinks before dinner, with the possible exception of the Meatball Appetizer, page 22, which is better suited for a cocktail party. If you do offer it before dinner, don't offer too many. If everyone loads up on these meatballs, no one really cares if dinner ever appears.

Artichoke Thistle Dip

You can play the "What is in this?" game with this recipe. No one will guess unless you tell. It's most unusual.

1 jar (6 ozs.) marinated artichoke hearts, undrained
1 cup sour cream
1 tsp. lemon juice
1/2 tsp. onion salt
1/4 tsp. garlic powder
dash cayenne pepper
assorted crackers and/or raw vegetables

Put artichokes in blender or food processor. Process or blend until completely smooth, scraping sides of blender or processor as necessary. Transfer puree to a small mixing bowl. Add remaining ingredients. Stir well. Refrigerate until thoroughly chilled. Serve with assorted raw vegetables, potato chips or crackers.

Lusty Italian Dip

This is best when prepared several hours ahead, but in an emergency can be prepared at the last minute.

1 pint sour cream
1 pkg. (1-1/2 ozs.) spaghetti sauce mix
1 tbs. instant minced onion
assorted crackers

13

Combine all ingredients in a mixing bowl. Stir until thoroughly mixed. Refrigerate for 2 hours before serving for best results. Serve with crackers.

> Hints: Thick yogurt can be substituted for part of the sour cream if you want to cut down on calories. If you are making a half recipe, don't forget to use only half the spaghetti sauce mix unless you like very spicy dips.

Serve these dips with an assortment of crackers and raw vegetables. Sesame or poppyseed crackers are a nice change of pace. Carrot sticks, celery sticks, cucumber slices, zucchini sticks, mushroom slices and cauliflower florets are great for dieters.

• Combine 1 pint of sour cream, 1 package (2-3/4 ozs.) dried Cream of Leek Soup Mix and 1 can (7 ozs.) chopped, drained clams in a bowl. Mix thoroughly. Refrigerate at least 1 hour before serving.

• Combine 1 pint sour cream 1 package (2-7/8 ozs.) dried Smoky Green Soup Mix and 1/2 cup grated sharp Cheddar cheese in a bowl. Mix thoroughly. Refrigerate at least 1 hour before serving.

People who love clams, love this and people who don't love clams, love it. The combination of colors makes it very attractive.

1 pkg. (8 ozs.) cream cheese, softened
1 tbs. fresh lemon juice
1 tsp. prepared mustard
1 tsp. Worchestershire sauce
2 tbs. fresh chopped parsley

2 tbs. instant minced onion
1 jar (2 ozs.) chopped pimentos
2 cans (7-1/2 ozs. each) minced clams
1/3 cup finely crushed crackers
1/2 cup finely chopped walnuts

In a mixing bowl, blend cream cheese with next 5 ingredients. Mix until smooth. Add pimentos, clams and cracker crumbs. Mix well. Shape into a log about 8 inches long. Roll in walnuts. Chill until firm. Serve with assorted crackers.

15

Boursin Favorite

If you have time to make only one appetizer to go with drinks, this should do it.

1 pkg. (8 ozs.) cream cheese, softened
2 cloves garlic, crushed
1 tsp. each caraway seed, basil, dill and fresh chopped chives
lemon pepper as coating for cheese

16   Use a fork to blend cream cheese with everything except lemon pepper. Pat into circular shape with sides about 1 inch high. Roll in lemon pepper. Chill. Serve with assorted crackers.

> Hint: This can be made several days ahead or just an hour before serving. For a large group, double the recipe. It goes fast. For something really special, try it on bagels.

Salmon Stuffed Eggs

This looks very impressive. Prepare a few more than you think you'll need.

8 hard-cooked eggs, halved lengthwise
2 tsp. Dijon-style mustard
2 tsp. Worcestershire sauce
2 tsp. lemon juice
1/2 tsp. salt
1/4 tsp. pepper
1/3 cup mayonnaise
1 can (7 ozs.) chunk-style salmon OR
    tuna fish, drained and mashed
fresh chopped parsley, for garnish (optional)
paprika, for garnish (optional)

18

Remove egg yolks from eggs and combine with rest of ingredients, except parsley and paprika. Spoon filling into egg white halves, or, for a professional touch pipe filling into egg white halves with a star-tipped bag. Garnish with parsley or paprika, if desired.

Hint: There is no trick to fixing perfect hard-cooked eggs. Place the desired amount of eggs in a saucepan. Cover them with cold water. Bring them to a rolling boil. Reduce the heat to simmer. Cook for 10 minutes, turning the eggs frequently. Immerse eggs immediately in cold water. Hard-cooked eggs should not be refrigerated until they are completely cooled; it toughens them.

The refrigerated biscuits I refer to as "Butter Gems" have different names depending on the brand. They are the many layered biscuits that come in a tube, found in the dairy section of your supermarket. They peel apart easily into thin layers.

1 tube of "Butter Gems"
Assortment of small pieces of: smoked sausage, halves of cocktail weiners, cubes of
   Cheddar cheese

20

Separate biscuits into layers. Place either sausage, weiners, OR cheese in the center of each layer. Pinch together on top. Place on cookie sheet. Bake at 400°F. about 10 minutes, or until brown. One tube of biscuits makes about 50 canapes.

> Hint: You can fill these canapes with crab, olives, chopped liver or anything else that appeals to you.

Do not overheat this mixture or it will separate. The savory flavor won't be affected, but its lovely appearance will!

When a recipe calls for drained marinated artichoke hearts, save the marinade to use as oil in salad dressings. Your salads will taste extra special.

2 jars (6 ozs. each) marinated artichoke hearts, drained
1 cup mayonnaise
1 cup grated Parmesan cheese OR grated Cheddar cheese
assorted crackers, corn chips and/or raw vegetables

21

Cut artichokes into small pieces. Combine artichokes, mayonnaise and cheese in an ovenproof mixing bowl. Blend well. Place in a 350ºF. oven for 10 minutes.

Meatball Appetizer

1 lb. very lean ground beef
1 tsp. Accent (optional)
salt and pepper
2 tbs. instant minced onion
1/2 cup soft breadcrumbs
1/4 cup milk
2 tbs. all-purpose flour

2 tbs. butter
3 tbs. molasses
3 tbs. prepared mustard
3 tbs. vinegar
1/4 cup catsup
1/4 tsp. thyme
wooden toothpicks

In a mixing bowl, blend meat with Accent, salt, pepper and minced onion. Use a light hand. Combine bread and milk. Add to meat. Toss lightly until well combined. Form into 3/4-inch balls* Roll in flour. Melt butter in large skillet over medium-high heat. Add meatballs and brown. Combine remaining ingredients. Add to meatballs. Simmer over low heat about 10 minutes, or until sauce thickens, stirring occasionally. Serve hot in a chafing dish with toothpicks. Makes about 50 meatballs.

*May be frozen at this point for up to 2 months. Allow to defrost before rolling in flour and browning.

Beefy Cheese Balls

1 pkg. (8 ozs.) cream cheese, softened
1 tsp. prepared horseradish
1 tsp. minced dried onion
1 jar (5 ozs.) dried chipped beef, shredded
pretzel sticks

   Mash cream cheese horseradish and onion together in a bowl. Chill for a half hour. Form into small balls about the size of a cherry. Roll in shredded chipped beef. Chill until ready to serve. Use pretzel sticks as toothpicks to skewer Cheese Balls. Makes about 50.

23

SOUPS

One of the few benefits of the rising cost of food is the increasing popularity of soups. In looking for less expensive ways to feed ourselves, we've found that soups are not only easy to prepare, but delicious and nutritious as well. A hearty soup can extend last night's leftovers into a full meal.

Soups are very forgiving. You can make errors and correct them without anyone ever knowing. Too thick? Add water. Too thin? A paste of cornstarch and water added to the soup can take care of that. If you don't have time to chop finely, as directed, cut everything into large, uneven pieces, cook it and give it a spin in the food processor. A cream soup!

Does the soup taste a little bland? Add a few herbs. Small pieces of leftover meat and vegetables can be chopped and added to the pot. Making soup gives you a chance to feel virtuous about "never throwing out leftovers." What's more, you've created a new soup.

This looks so spectacular, you feel a little guilty that it is so easy.

8 cups chicken broth
1/3 cup raw rice
3 eggs, separated
1/3 cup fresh lemon juice
salt and pepper
rind of 1 lemon, grated

26

In medium-sized saucepan bring chicken broth to boil. Sprinkle with rice, cover and cook over low heat for about 20 minutes or until rice is soft. Remove from heat and set aside. In a small bowl combine egg yolks, lemon juice and grated lemon rind. Gradually stir a little of the hot soup into the egg yolk mixture, stirring constantly (don't stir the egg yolks directly into the soup or mixture will curdle). Beat the egg whites until they hold definite peaks. Fold them into the hot soup. Add egg yolk-soup mixture to soup. Let it stand for 5 minutes before serving. Serves 6.

This simple Chinese soup complements any meal. For variety, substitute 1-1/2 cups diced celery for the corn. Cook for 15 minutes, or until celery is tender. And, instead of adding the eggs, stir in 1 cup of tightly packed fresh spinach leaves. Cook for 1 minute and serve.

6 cups well seasoned chicken broth
1 cup canned whole kernel corn, undrained
3/4 cup cooked chopped chicken
2 eggs, slightly beaten

Bring chicken broth to a boil in a saucepan. Puree corn in a food processor or blender. Add to broth along with chicken. Cook over low heat for 5 minutes. Add eggs to soup in a stream. Cook for another minute, stirring constantly. Serve immediately. Serves 6.

Sengalese Apple-Curry Soup

3 tbs. butter
1-1/2 cups tart apple, peeled, cored,
   and coarsely chopped
3/4 cup coarsely chopped onion
3 stalks celery, coarsely chopped
2 to 3 tsp. curry powder
salt and pepper
3 tbs. all-purpose flour
1 qt. canned chicken broth

3 whole cloves
1 large cinnamon stick
1 cup plain yogurt OR sour cream
2 tbs. minced green onion,
   for garnish (optional)
2 tbs. shredded cooked chicken,
   for garnish (optional)
1/2 cup tart apple, in matchstick pieces,
   for garnish (optional)

28

    Melt butter in saucepan over medium heat. Saute apples, onion and celery in butter until soft, about 8 minutes. Add curry, salt, pepper and flour. Saute 2 minutes more. Slowly add chicken broth, cloves and cinnamon stick. Reduce heat, cover and simmer 15 minutes. Cool slightly. Puree in food processor or blender if a smooth consistency is desired. Just before serving, place soup over medium heat. Add yogurt and stir until well blended. Garnish with minced onion, shredded chicken and matchstick apples if desired. Serves 6.

Cream of Carrot Soup

The carrots lend a lovely orange color to this soup.

1/4 cup butter
4 cups coarsely chopped carrots
3 large leeks, coarsely chopped
   (white part only) OR
1 cup coarsely chopped onion
1 tsp. sugar
salt and pepper
1 potato, peeled and coarsely chopped
1-1/2 cups water

3 cups half-and-half
grated black pepper, cayenne pepper
   and paprika
1 clove garlic, minced
2 tbs. brandy
croutons, for garnish (optional)
fresh chopped parsley, for garnish
   (optional)

Melt 1/4 cup butter in a large saucepan over medium heat. Add carrots and leeks. Saute about 6 minutes. Add sugar, salt, pepper, potato cubes and water. Cover and simmer until vegetables are just tender. Puree vegetables in a food processor or blender. Add half-and-half. Puree 30 seconds more. Add remaining seasonings, garlic and brandy. Simmer another 10 minutes to blend flavors, stirring occasionally. Serve hot, garnished with croutons and/or chopped parsley, if desired. Serves 6.

20 min.

 10 min.

Summer Squash Soup

2 tbs. oil (olive is best)
1/2 cup chopped onion
2 small cloves garlic, minced
2 zucchini (about the size of a large cucumber) thickly sliced
1/2 cup water
1/2 tsp. ginger
1 to 2 tsp. curry powder
salt and pepper
1/2 tsp. dried dill OR 2 tbs. fresh dill
1/2 bunch watercress (include a few stems)
1 pkg. (8 ozs.) cream cheese, softened and cut into 8 cubes
4 cups milk
4 tsp. lemon juice
watercress for garnish (optional)

Heat oil in saucepan to medium-high temperature. Saute onion and garlic 3 minutes. Add zucchini, water, ginger, curry, salt, pepper, dill and 1/2 bunch watercress. Simmer for 3 minutes; it should be undercooked. Pour contents of saucepan into food processor

30

or blender. Add remaining ingredients except watercress for garnish. Process or blend until smooth. Chill thoroughly. Chilling can be speeded up by placing mixture in freezer for 1/2 hour. Garnish with additional watercress just before serving, if desired. Serves 6.

Timesaver: If you're really pushed for time, you can omit the first step and put everything into the food processor raw. *You* might notice the difference, but no one else will.

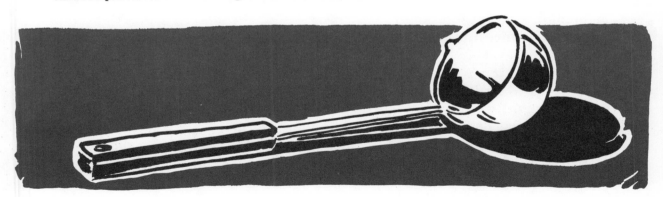

1/4 cup butter
1/2 cup chopped onion
1/2 lb. fresh mushrooms, halved
1 qt. chicken broth
3 tbs. butter
3 tbs. all-purpose flour
2 cups half-and-half
2 tbs. medium-dry sherry (optional)
1 tbs. fresh lemon juice (optional)

32

Melt 1/4 cup butter in saucepan over medium heat. Add onion and saute until soft. Add mushrooms. Saute 2 minutes more. Add chicken broth. Cover and simmer 10 minutes. Cool slightly. Puree for 30 seconds in food processor or blender if a very smooth consistency is desired. In a small skillet, melt 3 tablespoons butter over medium heat. Add flour. Cook 30 seconds. Add 1 cup of mushroom mixture. Add flour-mushroom mixture to the rest of the soup with the half-and-half. Simmer until very hot. Add sherry and lemon juice if desired. Serves 6.

Beer-Cheese Soup

This hearty soup is a great accompaniment to leftover meat or poultry.

1/2 cup butter
2 stalks EACH coarsely chopped
   celery and carrots
1 onion, quartered
1/2 cup all-purpose flour
1 quart chicken broth
1 quart chicken broth

1 tsp. dry mustard
2 tbs. grated Parmesan cheese
3/4 cup grated sharp Cheddar cheese
salt and pepper
1 tsp. sugar
1 can (12 ozs.) beer

34

In large saucepan, melt butter over medium heat. Add vegetables and saute about 5 minutes. Blend in flour. Add broth and mustard. Cook until vegetables are done, about 10 minutes, stirring occasionally. Cool slightly. Puree vegetable mixture in food processor or blender until smooth. Return to saucepan. Add cheeses, salt, pepper, sugar, and beer. Simmer 10 minutes to blend flavors. Serves 6.

3 tbs. butter
1/2 cup dry white wine
1/2 cup EACH diced leek, diced onion and diced celery
2 cups diced broccoli (stems and florets)
3 tbs. all-purpose flour
4 cups chicken stock
salt and pepper
1/2 tsp. thyme
1 cup light cream

35

Melt butter in saucepan over medium heat. Add wine and vegetables. Saute mixture for 5 minutes. Blend in flour and stock. Bring to a boil. Add seasonings. Simmer until vegetables are tender, about 10 minutes. Cool slightly. Place in blender or food processor. Blend or process until mixture is pureed. Add cream. Heat until piping, but do not allow to boil. Serves 6.

It's hard to believe that anything this simple can taste so good. This soup is the perfect filling for a thermos jug. It can be sipped out of a cup; no need for a spoon.

5 cups beef broth
3 cups canned vegetable juice cocktail
1 medium size onion stuck with 8 cloves
2 tbs. sugar
2 tsp. Worcestershire sauce
1/2 tsp. baking soda
1/4 tsp. Tabasco sauce
orange slices, for garnish (optional)

36

Combine all ingredients, except orange slices, in a large saucepan. Heat for 10 minutes. Do not boil. Discard onion. Garnish with orange slices, if desired. Serves 6.

If you are using canned soup that calls for the addition of water, use only half the water called for. To speed up the chilling process, place soup in freezer for 1/2 hour.

2 cans (14 ozs. each) ready-to-eat split pea soup
salt and pepper
1/2 tsp. curry powder
3 to 4 cups yogurt
2 to 3 tbs. fresh chopped chives
garlic croutons, for garnish (optional)

37

Combine split pea soup with salt, pepper and curry. Place over low heat until just at boiling point. Cool. Add yogurt and mix well. Chill. Just before serving add chopped chives. If desired, served with garlic croutons. Serves 6.

Cold Melon Soup

This soup is a wonderful way to use up those very ripe melons that have to be eaten right away. Freeze leftovers and serve in pretty glass bowls for a light and refreshing dessert.

2 cups EACH cubed ripe cantaloupe and honeydew melon
2 cups orange juice (fresh squeezed is best)
1/2 cup fresh lime juice (bottled juice won't taste the same)
3 to 4 tbs. honey, depending on sweetness of melons
2 cups white table wine (Sauterne OR Chablis)
1/2 cup Midori Melon Liqueur (optional)

38

Set aside 1 cup each of cantaloupe and honeydew melon. Place remaining melon in blender or food processor. Add juices and honey. Puree until smooth. This will have to be done in several batches. Mixture should be very thick. Transfer to large bowl. Add wine and liqueur until soup reaches proper consistency and desired flavor. Chill. At serving time add reserved melon balls. Pour into a glass salad or punch bowl for a dazzling presentation. Serves 6.

Hints: This soup can be prepared ahead and allowed to mellow for several hours, or can be served immediately, if pressed for time. Place in freezer for 1/2 hour to speed up chilling time. Adding more wine to the mixture turns this soup into a wonderful brunch-punch. For special occasions, substitute champagne for the wine. The taste will be similar, but the bubbles add a decidedly elegant touch. Omit the melon balls if you prepare it this way.

Even if you have a dozen recipes for Gazpacho and are convinced that there is nothing better than the one you've been using, try this one.

1 cucumber, peeled if the skin is waxed
5 green onions
1/2 large green pepper
2 stalks celery
1 large clove garlic, minced
1/4 cup EACH wine vinegar and fresh lemon juice
1/4 cup oil (olive, if possible)
1 quart jar Clamato Juice
1 can (1 lb.) tomato wedges OR sliced baby tomatoes, undrained
Salt and pepper
1 tsp. basil

Chop cucumber, green onions, green pepper and celery stalks coarsely. Place in food processor or blender and process for 30 seconds, until all vegetables are well chopped. Add wine vinegar, lemon juice and oil. Process 5 seconds more. Stir together vegetable

40

mixture, Clamato juice, tomatoes and seasonings to taste. Chill. Serves 6.

Hints: If time is short, place Gazpacho in the freezer for 1/2 hour to speed up the chilling process. If tomato wedges or baby tomatoes are unavailable, any high quality tomatoes, coarsely cut, will do. The others just look prettier.

FISH AND SEAFOOD

Some of us remember when certain kinds of seafood couldn't be even given away. No one would CHOOSE to eat mussels, or porgies, or bonito if they could get something else. Fish, in general, was an inexpensive answer to "What shall we eat?"

I knew that things had really changed when I saw a sign in a fishmarket that said, "major credit cards accepted." Now that some fish is more expensive than steak, it is important to take a little time to prepare it well. Fish and seafood are naturals for Fast and Delicious cooking. Since most of it can be eaten raw, there is certainly no need to present it rubbery and overcooked.

If you've ever wanted to experiment with herbs and spices, start with seafood. Basil, chervil, dill and tarragon combine wonderfully with it. Use a light hand at first; you don't want to overpower the delicate flavor of the fish.

Seafood is delicious, nutritious, and versatile. I wish I could also say inexpensive. But, alas, times have changed!

Swiss Sole Roll-Up

For most recipes, sole and flounder can be used interchangeably. It is certainly true of this one.

2 lbs. sole (6 fillets)
salt and pepper
1/2 tsp. EACH tarragon and dill
6 rectangles of Jarlsberg cheese, about 1 oz. each (other Swiss varieties will do, but the taste will be different)
1 can (8 ozs.) tomato-mushroom sauce
Parmesan cheese

Season fillets with salt, pepper, tarragon and dill. Place rectangle of cheese in center of fillet. Roll. Place seam side down, in buttered baking dish just large enough to hold fish. The rolls should be packed tightly together. Top with tomato-mushroom sauce. Bake at 350°F. for 15 minutes. Do not overcook. Sprinkle with Parmesan cheese. Bake 3 minutes longer. Serves 6.

This is a wonderful topping for fresh swordfish. It is also delicious with fresh salmon steaks.

1 jar (6 ozs.) marinated artichoke hearts
2 lbs. fresh swordfish steaks, or other fillets
3 tbs. fresh lemon juice
salt and pepper
1 cup sour cream (can substitute 1/2 cup thick plain yogurt for part of sour cream)
1/2 tsp. dill (optional)
1/2 cup cracker crumbs (Saltines are best)
2 tbs. butter

45

Drain artichoke hearts. Pour artichoke marinade into a large shallow baking dish. Place swordfish steaks in dish. Pour lemon juice, salt and pepper over them. Let stand about 15 minutes. If pushed for time this step can be omitted. Top with artichoke hearts. Spoon sour cream over fish. Sprinkle with dill and crumbs. Dot with butter. Bake uncovered at 375°F. for 25 minutes, or until fish flakes when prodded with a fork. Serves 6.

Sole With Almond Crust

This unusual combination works very well with any lean white fish. It combines beautifully with rice, roasted potatoes or French bread.

2 lbs. fillet of sole
salt and pepper
1 cup sour cream
2 tbs. lemon juice
2 tbs. Worcestershire sauce
1 tsp. dill

1 tsp. onion powder
1 cup very finely chopped blanched almonds
2 tbs. butter
2 tbs. oil
lemon slices, for garnish (optional)
chopped parsley, for garnish (optional)

46

Sprinkle fish lightly with salt and pepper. Mix sour cream with lemon juice, Worcestershire, dill and onion powder. Coat fish with this mixture on both sides. Press chopped nuts into fish. In large skillet, heat oil and butter over medium heat. Saute fish quickly until golden on both sides. Garnish with lemon slices and parsley. Serves 6.

This is a perfect sauce for poached salmon or any other poached fish. It can be used for a buffet as a mask for a whole fish. It is not only delicious but has an appealing color. It keeps well for several days in the refrigerator.

1/2 cup mayonnaise
1/2 cup sour cream
1 pkg. (8 ozs.) cream cheese, softened
2 tbs. capers
1 tsp. mustard
3 tbs. chopped instant onion (or fresh)
2 tbs. chopped anchovy fillets
3 dashes Worcestershire sauce
2 tbs. chili sauce
2 tbs. fresh lemon juice

Place all ingredients in food processor or blender. Process or blend until smooth. Makes enough for a 4 to 5 pound fish.

47

This is a marinade that becomes a sauce for the fish.

1 small onion, halved
1 clove garlic
1/3 cup vegetable oil
salt and pepper
juice of 1 lemon (use fresh only)
combination of herbs (tarragon, dill, basil, chives, parsley),
    use 1/2 teaspoon each of two or three
2 lbs. fish fillets
paprika

48

Place onion and garlic in food processor. Process until liquified. Gradually add oil while processor is in motion until mixture is consistency of mayonnaise. All oil may not be needed. Add salt, pepper, lemon juice and choice of herbs. Process 3 seconds. Marinate fish fillets with mixture in a shallow baking pan about 1/2 hour. Place baking pan under broiler; do not remove marinade. Broil until fish flakes when prodded with a fork. Sprinkle with paprika. Serves 6.

Canned fish can be turned into a satisfying meal in just a few minutes. No need to use solid pack fish; chunk style works just as well and is less expensive.

1-1/2 lbs. canned salmon OR tuna fish
   (3 small cans), flaked
3 tbs. butter
3 tbs. all-purpose flour
1-1/2 cups milk
1 can (8-1/2 ozs.) water chestnuts,
   drained and sliced
3 tsp. Dijon-style mustard

3 tbs. dry sherry
salt and pepper
1/2 tsp. EACH dill and tarragon
1/2 cup chopped green onion
4 drops Tabasco sauce
3 tbs. Parmesan cheese
3 tbs. breadcrumbs
paprika

49

Drain salmon, reserving liquid. Melt butter in medium skillet over medium heat. Add flour and stir until well blended. Slowly whisk in milk and reserved salmon liquid. Cook until thick. Combine sauce with salmon and remaining ingredients, except cheese, breadcrumbs and paprika. place mixture in lightly buttered shallow 9-inch baking dish. Combine cheese and breadcrumbs. Sprinkle on top of casserole. Dust with paprika. Bake, uncovered for 15 minutes at 425°F. Serves 6.

Salmon Steaks Teriyaki

Fresh salmon is so succulent, it seems its flavor cannot be improved upon. However, this marinade actually seems to enhance its flavor. It vastly improves the taste of frozen salmon.

6 salmon steaks, 1/4 to 1/2 lbs. each
1/4 cup vegetable oil
2 tbs. fresh lemon juice
2 tbs. dry sherry
2 tbs. soy sauce

1/2 tsp. dry mustard
1/2 tsp. grated fresh ginger OR
   ginger powder
1 clove garlic, minced

50

Place steaks in shallow dish, just large enough to hold them. Combine remaining ingredients. Pour over steaks. Marinate at room temperature for 1 hour or overnight. Drain and reserve marinade. Place steaks on buttered broiler pan. Broil 3 inches from heat for 5 minutes, brushing with marinade several times. Turn. Broil a few more minutes, or until fish flakes when prodded with a fork. Serves 6.

Hint: remaining marinade may be reused. It keeps well in the refrigerator for up to 3 weeks. Try it on other types of fish too—swordfish is good.

Though fresh oysters are best, the oysters that come in a jar give very satisfactory results. If you've had both, you will know the difference, but no one else will.

1/4 cup butter
3/4 cup finely chopped onion
2 packages (12 ozs. each)
   frozen chopped spinach,
   defrosted and squeezed dry
2 tbs. all-purpose flour
1 cup sour cream (can substitute 1/2 cup
   thick plain yogurt for part of sour cream)

salt and pepper
24 large oysters
1/2 cup dry sherry
1/2 cup grated Parmesan cheese OR
   grated sharp Cheddar cheese
paprika

52

Melt butter over medium heat in a skillet. Saute onion in melted butter until golden. Add spinach and flour. Cook another two minutes, stirring. Add sour cream, salt and pepper. Stir to blend. Remove from heat. Cover an oven proof plate with spinach mixture to about 1/2 inch deep. Arrange oysters on top. Sprinkle oysters with sherry and cheese. Sprinkle with little more salt and paprika. Bake at 400°F. for about 20 minutes. Do not overcook. Serve directly from plate. Serves 6.

Shrimp, Pea and Mushroom Stir-Fry

This stir-fry dish can be varied in many ways: you can substitute pea-pods for frozen peas and water chestnuts for mushrooms; the shrimp can be replaced with slivers of chicken breast; and if you have some celery or green pepper that needs eating, slice it on the diagonal and just throw it in. Although the recipe calls for a wok, a large heavy skillet works just as well.

1 tbs. cornstarch
1 tsp. EACH salt, sugar and
    fresh grated ginger
3/4 cup chicken broth
2 tbs. soy sauce
1 large clove garlic, crushed

1/4 cup peanut oil
3/4 lb. fresh mushrooms, sliced
1 package (10 ozs.) frozen peas, defrosted
1/4 cup minced green onions
1-1/2 lbs. fresh shrimp,
    peeled and deveined

53

Blend cornstarch with salt, sugar, fresh grated ginger, chicken broth, soy sauce and garlic. Set aside. Pre-heat wok 3 minutes over high heat. Add oil and mushrooms. Stir-fry over high heat 1 minute. Add peas and onions. Stir-fry 2 minutes. Add shrimp. Stir-fry 2 to 3 minutes, until just done. Do not overcook. Add chicken broth mix and stir until thick. Serve immediately with steamed rice. Serves 6.

Back in "the good ol' days" . . . when shrimp was inexpensive, we enjoyed this dish frequently. It is fantastic eating.

18 to 24 large (jumbo are better) shrimp
2 tbs. all-purpose flour
1/4 cup butter
1/4 cup olive oil

Drawn Butter Sauce
4 tbs. butter
2 tbs. all-purpose flour
salt and freshly ground pepper
2 tsp. fresh lemon juice
1 cup hot water
2 tbs. finely chopped garlic
1/4 cup fresh chopped parsley
1/2 tsp. oregano

Dust shrimp generously with flour. In a flat broiling pan, melt 1/4 cup butter under broiler. Add oil and heat until bubbly. Place shrimp in pan, coat with butter-oil mixture. Broil under heat about 3 minutes. Shrimp will not be done. Prepare Drawn Butter Sauce. Melt 2 tablespoons butter in saucepan over medium heat. Add flour, salt and

pepper. Stir well. Whisk in lemon juice and water. Cook about 5 minutes. Add remaining 2 tablespoons butter and stir until melted. Just before removing from heat, add garlic, parsley and oregano to sauce. Heat about 1 minute. Pour over broiled shrimp and stir until shrimp are coated. Return shrimp to broiler and broil under high heat 3 to 4 minutes, or just until shrimp turn pink. Serve with plenty of French bread to soak up that marvelous sauce. Serves 6.

Fresh shrimp are preferable, but frozen raw shrimp work very well, and they are already deveined. Be careful not to overcook the shrimp or they will toughen. They are done the moment they turn pink.

56

2 lbs. raw shrimp, shelled and deveined
1/2 tsp. salt
dash pepper
1 tbs. honey
2 tbs. soy sauce
1 tbs. dry sherry
3 tbs. vegetable oil
2 tbs. minced scallions, for garnish (optional)

Place shrimp in a flat baking dish. Blend together salt, pepper, honey, soy sauce and sherry. Let marinate about 15 minutes. Add oil and mix thoroughly. Bake at 375°F. for 10 minutes. Sprinkle with scallions, if desired. Serves 6.

Hint: Serve with rice and stir-fried vegetables.

Purists say, "Please!, no cheese with this; it masks the delicate flavor of the clams." But I believe the version with cheese is by far the most popular.

1/4 cup olive oil
1/2 cup butter
3 cloves garlic, finely chopped
   (to taste)
1/4 cup finely chopped parsley
1 tsp. basil
1/2 tsp. oregano
pinch dry crushed red pepper

salt and pepper
2 cans (7 ozs. each) chopped clams
   undrained
1 can tomato sauce (optional,
   use only if red sauce is preferred
3 tbs. grated Parmesan cheese (optional)
cooked Fettucine noodles to serve 6.

57

In a saucepan heat oil and butter over medium heat. Add remaining ingredients except clams, tomato sauce and cheese. Simmer about 5 minutes. Add clams and tomato sauce. Simmer 5 minutes longer. Do not overcook. Toss with noodles. Serve with Parmesan cheese, if desired. Serves 6.

CHICKEN

A most pleasant childhood memory is going with my mother to the butcher to buy a chicken. Though they all looked the same to me, she spent some time choosing the right bird. She always asked for a freshly-killed chicken. She felt its breast, questioned the butcher about its pedigree, and looked under the feathers.

After the selection was made, she grabbed the chicken by the legs and brought it into the back room to the "chicken-flicker." In the middle of a mountain of feathers sat a shapeless old woman with large magical hands that quickly "dressed" our chicken. Whenever I hear the expression "naked as a plucked chicken," I recall the pang I felt to see our bird in its denuded state. The woman always handed me a chicken foot, also for good luck, which my mother always added to the soup.

Sad to say, the meal that resulted was not worth the effort. My mother's cooking repertoire consisted of two ways of preparing chicken: boiled and roasted. Both resulted in tough and tasteless birds.

My own collection consists of over 100 recipes, including one that makes chicken taste like veal (see Chicken Piccata, page 76). I love being able to choose from my many recipes. But once in a while, I remember my trips to the butcher as a child and I wish I could find one that would let me look under the feathers and give me a chicken foot . . . for good luck.

Lemon Chicken With Spinach

one 3 lb. fryer, cut into serving pieces OR
use thighs, drumsticks and wings
salt, pepper, garlic power and
onion powder to taste
1 cup chicken broth OR 2 chicken
bouillon cubes in 1-1/2 cups boiling water
1/4 cup sugar
1/4 cup fresh lemon juice

1 tbs. water
1 tbs. dry sherry
2 tbs. soy sauce
2-1/2 tsp. cornstarch
1 lb. fresh spinach
bean sprouts
chopped scallions

60

Place cut up chicken on baking sheet. Sprinkle with salt, pepper, garlic powder and onion powder. Bake at 350°F. until done, about 40 minutes. Combine broth, sugar, lemon juice, water, sherry, soy sauce and cornstarch in a saucepan. Stir over medium heat until thick. Wash spinach and discard thick stems. Dry thoroughly (in a salad spinner, if you have one). Shred spinach and place on large serving platter. Sprinkle fresh bean sprouts on top of the spinach. Top with baked chicken, then add thickened sauce. Sprinkle with chopped scallions. Serves 4 to 6.

Manhattan Chicken

This combination is unusual and delicious; and it couldn't be easier.

one 3 lb. fryer, cut into serving pieces OR
  use chicken parts
salt, pepper, onion powder,
  garlic powder to taste
1/4 cup butter
1/2 cup sliced celery
1/2 cup sliced fresh mushrooms

1/3 cup chopped onion
1/2 can (10-3/4 ozs.)
  condensed Manhattan Clam Chowder
1/2 can (10-3/4 ozs.)
  condensed Cream of Mushroom Soup
1/4 cup dry sherry
1/4 cup water

61

Sprinkle chicken with salt, pepper, onion powder and garlic powder. Place on a buttered baking sheet. Bake at 425°F. for about 20 minutes. Meanwhile, in a large skillet, melt butter over medium heat. Saute vegetables until limp, about 8 minutes. Remove vegetables from skillet. Place browned chicken in skillet. Combine vegetables with rest of ingredients. Pour over chicken. Cover and simmer 20 minutes, stirring occasionally. Serve with rice. Serves 4 to 6.

Baked Chicken With Sour Cream

This dish becomes extra special when served with homemade noodles. If you don't want to make your own, buy some at a local delicatessen. For a really colorful dish, try using green fettucini.

flour seasoned with salt and pepper
1/2 tsp. EACH rosemary and paprika
1 tsp. grated lemon rind
3 lbs. chicken pieces
1/2 cup water
1/4 cup Madeira wine (or less, to taste)
2 tbs. butter
2 tbs. all-purpose flour
1/2 cup sour cream
chopped parsley, for garnish (optional)

62

Place seasoned flour, rosemary, paprika and grated lemon rind in a plastic bag. Toss to mix. Shake chicken pieces in mixture until coated. Shake off excess flour. Place pieces on a lightly buttered baking sheet. Broil until brown on all sides, about 5 minutes.

If you are in a hurry, you can omit the broiling step. The flavor, however, is a little better if the chicken is broiled. Place chicken pieces in a shallow casserole. Combine water and Madeira. Pour over chicken. Bake uncovered 45 minutes at 350°F. Remove chicken and place on warm serving platter. Measure 3/4 cups of the pan juices and set aside. In a skillet, over medium heat, melt butter. Add flour. Allow to bubble 30 seconds. Add pan juices and stir until thick. Stir 1/2 cup of the thickened mixture into sour cream. Stir the sour cream mixture into the remaining sauce. Mix carefully. Do not allow mixture to boil or sour cream might curdle. Spoon over chicken. Garnish with chopped parsley, if desired. Serves 4 to 6.

Baked Chicken All-In-One

1/2 cup water
1/2 can (10-3/4 ozs.) Cream of Mushroom Soup
1/2 pkg. (1-1/2 ozs.) dried onion soup
1/4 cup dry sherry
2/3 cup raw rice
3 lbs. small chicken parts (wings, drumsticks, thighs, breasts cut into quarters)
salt and pepper

Stir together all ingredients except chicken. Place in a 13 x 9 x 2-inch baking dish. Place chicken pieces on top. Salt and pepper lightly. Cover. Bake for 35 minutes at 350°F. Uncover and bake an additional 15 minutes, or until tender. Serves 4 to 6.

This recipe can be served hot or at room temperature.

one 3-pound chicken cut into small pieces,
  OR use thighs, drumsticks and wings
1/4 cup fresh lime juice (fresh is important)
1/3 cup rum (white is preferable)
3 tbs. soy sauce

2 large cloves garlic, crushed
all-purpose flour
lime wedges, for garnish (optional)

65

Toss chicken with lime juice. In a plastic bag, combine rum, soy sauce and garlic. Add chicken and lime juice and let mixture marinate in refrigerator for several hours or overnight. Drain. Dredge chicken in flour, shaking off excess. You can omit the flour step if you are in a hurry. Place chicken in a shallow pan. Bake at 350ºF. for 45 minutes, or until done. Serve with lime wedges if desired. Serves 4 to 6.

Timesaver: If you don't have time to marinate the chicken for several hours, marinating it for an hour (or less) at room temperature works almost as well. If you do that, the flavor of the recipe is improved by making the marinade into a sauce. To do this, add 1-1/2 tablespoons of cornstarch to 1/4 cup water. Mix until smooth. Add to marinade. Heat in a saucepan until mixture thickens and is bubbly. Serve as a sauce with the chicken.

Chinese Barbecued Chicken

1/2 cup soy sauce
2-1/2 tsp. oil (peanut, if possible)
1/2 tsp. dry mustard
1 tbs. fresh grated ginger OR
   1 tsp. ginger powder
1/4 tsp. salt,
dash pepper
1/2 tsp. onion powder

2 cloves garlic, chopped
1/4 cup dry sherry
one 3 lb. fryer, cut
   into serving pieces
cooked noodles to serve 4 to 6
fresh chopped parsley, for garnish
   (optional)

66

Mix together all ingredients except chicken, noodles and parsley. Brush chicken with mixture. Let stand 30 minutes, brushing several times more. Place chicken on baking sheet and bake at 400°F. for 40 to 50 minutes, basting every 15 minutes. Chicken should be brown and crisp. Serve with noodles. Garnish with parsley, if desired. Serves 4 to 6.

Hint: marinade may be reused, simply store it in the refrigerator for up to 3 weeks. Or, toss remaining marinade with noodles and parsley and serve with chicken.

This dish has just a few ingredients, but the combination is very pleasing. It is especially good if you use a variety of cheeses.

Toss little bits of leftover cheese into a plastic bag. Store them in the freezer. When you make things calling for cheese, shred some from your collection. You'll be amazed how tasty the combination is.

one 3-lb. fryer, cut into serving pieces, or use chicken parts
salt, pepper, onion powder, garlic powder to taste
2 tbs. butter
2 tbs. minced green onion
2 tbs. all-purpose flour
1 cup half-and-half
1 tsp. Dijon-style mustard
1/2 cup grated Swiss cheese or a mixture of Swiss, Cheddar, and Parmesan
1 tbs. breadcrumbs

68

Sprinkle chicken with salt, pepper, onion powder and garlic powder. Place on a lightly buttered baking sheet. Bake at 350°F. for 45 minutes, or until done. Meanwhile, make sauce. Melt butter in a saucepan over medium heat. Add onions and saute until done. Stir in flour. Whisk in half-and-half. Add mustard and 1/4 cup cheese. Place cooked chicken on an oven-proof platter. Pour sauce over chicken. Combine bread-crumbs and remaining cheese. Sprinkle on top of sauce. Add a few tablespoons pan drippings on top. Broil until lightly browned. Watch carefully; it only takes a few minutes. Serves 6.

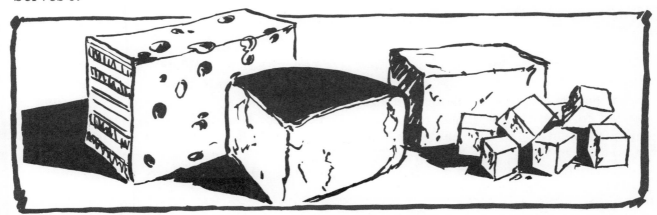

This is a Greek dish. It combines perfectly with French bread, Sweet-Sour Eggplant (page 152) and a romaine lettuce salad tossed with oil and wine vinegar and topped with crumbled Feta cheese.

6 chicken breast halves, unboned and unskinned
1/2 cup olive oil
1/2 cup fresh lemon juice
3 cloves garlic, chopped

2 tsp. oregano
1/2 tsp. thyme
salt and pepper

Arrange chicken breasts in a pan just large enough to hold them. Place remaining ingredients in blender or food processor. Process 30 seconds. Pour over chicken. Let stand (covered) in refrigerator overnight, or an hour at room temperature. If you are pushed for time, just marinate as long as possible. Drain; reserve marinade. Place chicken breasts on broiler pan, skin side down. Broil for 5 minutes. Brush with marinade once while broiling. Reduce heat to 375°F. Bake for 20 minutes. Turn chicken, skin side up; brush again. Turn heat up to 550°F. and broil until golden brown, about 5 minutes. Serve with marinade. Serves 6.

I had the pleasure of watching an Italian grandmother prepare this recipe. She couldn't tell me the exact quantities of any of the ingredients she used. She said she was not taught to cook that way. This is my version of her old family favorite.

1-1/2 cups all-purpose flour
salt and pepper
2 tsp. EACH basil and oregano
1 fryer, cut into serving pieces
2 tbs. olive oil
1 cup chopped onion

2 cloves garlic, minced
1 can (1 lb.) tomatoes
1 tbs. minced fresh basil or 1 tsp. dried
1/2 tsp. sugar
salt and pepper
grated Parmesan and Romano cheese

71

In a bag, toss together flour, salt, pepper, 2 teaspoons EACH basil and oregano. Shake chicken pieces in bag, 2 at a time. Place on lightly buttered baking sheet. Meanwhile, heat olive oil in skillet over medium-low heat. Saute onion and garlic until limp. Remove from heat. Place chicken in casserole dish. Cover with sauteed onions and garlic. Mix tomatoes with basil, sugar, salt and pepper. Cover and bake at 350°F. for 30 minutes. Serve with small pasta and grated cheese.   Serves 4 to 6.

Oven-Fried Parmesan Chicken

This is a very different kind of oven-fried chicken. It is also delicious cold.

1/2 cup melted butter
2 cloves garlic, crushed
2 tsp. Dijon-style mustard
   (more if you like a strong taste)
1 tsp. Worchestershire sauce
1 cup breadcrumbs (can substitute
   part cornmeal)

1/2 cup grated Parmesan cheese
salt and pepper
1/2 tsp. oregano
2 tbs. fresh chopped parsley
3 lbs. chicken drumsticks and thighs
   OR other small pieces
paprika

72

In a large shallow dish combine melted butter with garlic, mustard and Worcestershire sauce. In plastic bag, combine breadcrumbs with remaining ingredients, except paprika. Dip chicken pieces in butter mixture and then shake in plastic bag, coating well. Arrange pieces in another large shallow baking dish. Pour remaining butter over them. Bake at 350°F. for 1 hour, or until done, basting occasionally. Just before serving, sprinkle with paprika. Serves 6.

Hot Chicken Salad Supreme

This is a wonderful way to use up leftover chicken or turkey in a dish that doesn't taste like "leftovers."

2 cups cooked rice
3 cups diced cooked chicken OR turkey
2 cups diced celery
1/3 cup finely chopped dill pickles
1/3 cup chopped walnuts
1/4 cup chopped green onion

salt and pepper
1/2 tsp. EACH tarragon and dill
1 cup mayonnaise
1 cup grated sharp Cheddar cheese
1 cup crushed potato chips OR cereal
  (wheat flakes or rice flakes)

73

In a mixing bowl, stir together everything except cheese and potato chips. Pour mixture into a 2-1/2-quart baking dish. In a bowl, mix cheese and chips. Sprinkle over top of casserole. Bake at 350°F. 20 minutes, or until hot and bubbly. Serves 6.

Don't be put off by the combination of ingredients in this sauce. Catsup and pineapple juice may seem a little odd, but the whole thing together is very special.

2 tbs. butter
1/4 cup EACH chopped onion and
   green pepper
1 cup sliced carrots
1/3 cup catsup
1/2 cup pineapple juice
2 tbs. vinegar
2 tbs. firmly packed brown sugar

garlic powder, salt and pepper to taste
1 tbs. soy sauce
dash Tabasco sauce
1/2 tsp. ginger powder
1/2 cup pineapple chunks
one 3-lb. chicken, cut into serving pieces
1 banana, peeled and quartered (optional)

74

Melt butter in skillet over medium heat. Saute onion, green pepper and carrots about 5 minutes in butter. Stir in remaining ingredients, except chicken and bananas. Stir until thoroughly heated. Arrange chicken in a large buttered baking dish. Pour sauce on top. Bake covered for 30 minutes at 350ºF. Uncover and bake an additional 20 minutes, or until chicken and carrots are done. Add bananas at this point, if desired. Serve with rice. Serves 4 to 6.

This is one of those recipes where you just throw it together. It goes with rice or noodles. The sauce is delicious.

1-1/2 lbs. chicken breasts,
   skinned and boned
1-1/2 cups dry red wine
1/2 cup soy sauce
1/2 cup vegetable oil
3 cloves garlic, coarsely chopped
1/2 cup water

2 tsp. ginger powder OR
   2 tbs. fresh, grated
1/2 tsp. oregano
2 tbs. firmly packed brown sugar
3 tbs. cornstarch
3 tbs. water

75

Slightly flatten chicken breasts. You can omit this step if you are in a hurry. Combine remaining ingredients and mix well. Place breasts in a buttered baking dish just big enough to hold them. Pour sauce on top. Bake, uncovered, at 375ºF. for 20 to 25 minutes or until done. Remove chicken to serving platter. Pour sauce over chicken. Serves 6.

Chicken Piccata

This is an adaptation of veal piccata. Sometimes even very knowledgeable people can't tell the difference.

2 lbs. boned and skinned chicken breasts
1/2 cup all-purpose flour seasoned with salt and pepper
1/2 tsp. EACH paprika and tarragon
1/4 cup butter
2 tbs. olive oil
1/4 cup dry Madeira OR dry sherry (can use water in an emergency)
3 tbs. fresh lemon juice
lemon slices
3 tbs. capers (can omit, but it detracts from the dish)
1/4 cup chopped fresh parsley, for garnish (optional)

Try to get your butcher to pound the chicken breasts for you. If you have to do it yourself, place breasts between two sheets of waxed paper and pound until they are 1/4-inch thick. Toss seasoned flour, paprika and tarragon together in a plastic bag. Add breasts, shake until well coated. Shake off excess. Heat butter and oil in a large skillet over medium heat until they bubble. Saute breasts a few at a time, 2 to 3 minutes on each side. DO NOT OVERCOOK. Drain on paper towels. Keep warm. To remaining butter-oil mixture in pan add Madeira. Stir to loosen any brown bits sticking to bottom of skillet. Add lemon juice and heat a few minutes. A few minutes before serving, add chicken and lemon slices. Heat until sauce thickens. Add capers. Sprinkle with chopped parsley, if desired and serve. Serves 6.

Hint: Serve with Almond Noodles, page 144 and Rum Chocolate Mousse, page 170.

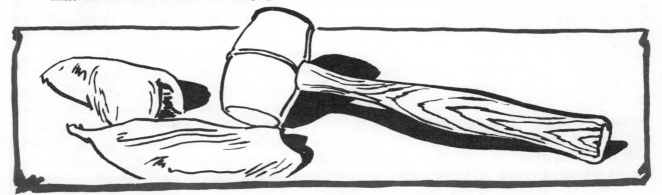

Chicken A La Madeline

This unusual dish comes from Lyon. It was a French family secret.

2 lbs. boned and skinned chicken breasts
1/2 cup all-purpose flour seasoned with
   salt and pepper
3 tbs. butter
2 tbs. olive oil
4 shallots, minced
2 cloves garlic, minced

1/4 lb. mushrooms, sliced
1/2 cup good quality wine vinegar
1/2 tsp. sugar
salt and pepper
1/2 tsp. tarragon
2 to 3 tbs. tomato paste
1 cup sour cream

78

It saves time if you can get your butcher to pound the chicken breasts. If you have to do it yourself, place breasts between two sheets of waxed paper and pound until they are 1/4-inch thick. Put seasoned flour in a plastic bag. Shake chicken breasts in bag to coat. Shake off excess flour. Combine butter and oil in a large skillet over medium heat. Saute chicken breasts a few at a time, 2 minutes on each side. They cook quickly, so be careful not to overcook. Remove chicken from skillet when lightly browned on both sides. Add more oil or butter to skillet if needed. Saute shallots, garlic and mushrooms. Add vinegar. Scrape all brown bits from bottom of pan into sauce. Add sugar, seasonings and tomato paste to skillet. If sauce seems too thick add up to a cup of water. Return chicken to skillet. Cover with sauce and cook about 5 minutes, in covered skillet, over low heat. Do not overcook. Add sour cream and mix into sauce. Heat just enough to warm sour cream thoroughly, about 3 minutes. Serve immediately. Serves 6.

Hint: Serve this dish with French bread, a green vegetable and salad. Lemon Pie-Cake, page 160, is an excellent dessert for this meal. The entire meal can be prepared in an hour.

For something truly spectacular, substitute veal scallops for the chicken breasts. Substitute tarragon vinegar for the wine vinegar.

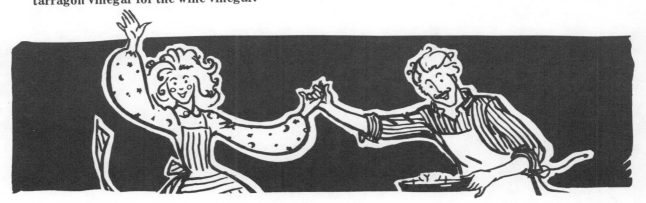

MEATS

There are fashions in foods just as in clothing or hair styles. For years the mainstay of the American diet has been meat and potatoes. Now, if people are on a meat and potatoes diet, many of them won't admit it. We are constantly being told that we will live healthier lives by eating less meat. Is it just a coincidence that this new awareness comes at a time when meat has become very expensive? Perhaps if steak were suddenly $1.00 a pound again, many people would decide that it isn't so unhealthy, after all.

It is important that we enjoy what we eat. Life is too short to be worried about our health all the time. If you follow the food fashions you know that opinions can change very fast. Next week someone may "prove" that the anti-meat people are all wrong and that we must have meat for strong blood or thick hair. But, before the final decision is in, you can, if you wish, cut down on the meat in some of these recipes by increasing the amounts of vegetables. The result will be just as fast; just as delicious.

Even people who don't like ham enjoy this dish.

2 cans (11 ozs. each) mandarin oranges, drained
2 cups cooked rice
1/3 cup mayonnaise
3 tbs. EACH chopped pecans, parsley and green onions
12 large slices boiled ham
1/2 cup orange marmalade
2 tbs. fresh lemon juice
1/2 tsp. ginger

82

Reserve 12 orange sections. Toss together remaining oranges, rice, mayonnaise, pecans, parlsey and green onions. Place a large spoonful of mixture in center of each slice of ham. Roll slices. Place seam side down in a baking dish just large enough to hold rolls. Combine marmalade, lemon juice and ginger. Brush rolls with this mixture. Bake at 350°F. for 25 minutes. Garnish with reserved oranges. Serves 6.

Szeged Pork Goulash

This is a Hungarian dish. Although it seems exotic and looks impressive, it is very easy to prepare. The sweet Hungarian paprika is essential for the success of this dish. It is available in many delicatessens or gourmet shops.

2 tbs. vegetable oil
1-1/2 cups chopped onion
2 lbs. lean pork shoulder, cut in 1/2-inch cubes
2 tsp. sweet Hungarian paprika
salt and pepper
1/2 tsp. caraway seeds (or to taste)

1 small can tomato paste
1/2 cup water
1/2 tsp. sugar
2 large raw potatoes, grated
1 lb. sauerkraut, drained
1 cup sour cream

Heat oil to medium temperature in skillet. Add onions. Cook until golden brown. Add pork. Cook until it loses its pink color, about 5 minutes. Add remaining ingredients, except sour cream. Mix well. Cover and cook slowly, 20 to 30 minutes, until pork is done and potatoes are tender. Just before serving, add sour cream and heat through. Do not let sour cream boil or it may curdle. Serves 6. This is an all-in-one dish. Toss a salad and you have a complete meal.

83

The colors and textures combine to make this a most delicious and attractive dish suitable for company. For fun, complete the meal with green tea.

3 large green peppers, cut
   into 6 pieces each
2 lbs. lean pork (shoulder),
   cut in 1/2-inch cubes
2 tbs. vegetable oil
1/2 tsp. salt
dash pepper
2 cloves garlic, minced
1 package (6 ozs.) frozen peapods,
   thawed (optional)

6 slices canned pineapple,
   drained and cut into 6 pieces each
3 tbs. cornstarch
2 tbs. soy sauce
1/2 cup rice vinegar
   OR white vinegar
1/2 cup sugar
2/3 cup chicken bouillon
1/2 cup chopped green onions
steamed rice to serve 6

Cook cut green peppers in boiling water 5 minutes. Drain. In large skillet warm oil over medium heat. Add pork, salt and pepper. Saute over medium heat about 8 minutes, until pork is done. Add garlic, saute another minute. Add chicken bouillon, peapods and cook about 4 minutes. Add pineapple and green peppers. Combine rest of ingredients,

84

except green onion. Stir until smooth. Add to skillet and stir until thick, about 2 minutes. Top with green onions. Serve immediately with hot boiled rice. Serves 6.

Hint: For a special treat, use fresh peapods and fresh slices of pineapple.

When all else fails, you can always turn to this. You can teach a 10-year-old to do it, which gives you some idea of how difficult it is. Barbecue on hamburger buns is a wonderful children's birthday party meal.

2 tbs. vegetable oil
1-1/2 cups chopped onion
2 cloves garlic, minced
2 lbs. ground beef chuck
salt and pepper
1 jar (14 ozs.) chili sauce (Bennett's is the preferred brand, but another will do)
6 hamburger buns

86

In a large skillet heat oil to medium temperature. Saute onion, garlic and beef in oil until beef loses color. Drain if too much fat appears. Add chili sauce, salt and pepper. Heat through, about 5 minutes. Serve on warmed hamburger buns. Serves 6.

Souperburger Italiano

2 tbs. vegetable oil
2 lbs. ground beef chuck
1 cup chopped onion
2 cloves garlic, minced
1 tsp. EACH oregano and basil
salt and pepper
1 can (10-3/4 ozs.) minestrone soup, undiluted
1/3 cup catsup
1/3 cup water
6 hamburger buns, cut in half
1/2 cup grated Parmesan cheese

87

Heat oil to medium temperature in skillet. Add meat, onion and garlic. Simmer until onion and garlic are limp. Add rest of ingredients except hamburger buns and cheese. Simmer 5 minutes. While mixture is cooking, toast and butter buns. Divide mixture on buns. Top with grated Parmesan. Broil for 1 minute or until brown. Watch carefully or it will burn. Serves 6.

This sandwich filling is a meal in itself. Proportions of sausage and vegetables can be varied to suit individual taste.

Sweet Fried Pepper and Onion can be found in the Italian section of your supermarket or a delicatessen.

Try serving pieces of this as an appetizer too.

88

1 lb. sweet Italian sausage
1/2 lb. hot Italian sausage
3 cloves garlic, minced
1 large onion, chopped
4 stalks celery, coarsely chopped
1 green pepper, chopped (optional)

1 jar Sweet Fried Pepper and Onion
1 tsp. salt
1/2 tsp. black pepper
1/2 tsp. oregano
1/2 lb. cubed Mozzarella cheese
Pita (pocket) bread

Remove casing from sausages. Saute in skillet over medium heat for 10 minutes. Drain. Add raw vegetables. Saute 5 minutes. Add jar Sweet Fried Pepper and Onion and seasonings. Cool 15 minutes (important). Add cubed Mozzarella. Chill for 10 minutes. Serve in warm pita bread. Makes 6 sandwiches.

1/4 cup vegetable oil
2 lbs. lean ground beef (can substitute part pork sausage)
1 cup minced onion
2 cloves garlic, minced
3 cans (8 ozs. each) tomato sauce
1 cup Burgundy wine
1 tsp. EACH basil and oregano
1/2 tsp. EACH garlic powder and rosemary
1 tbs. sugar
1/2 lb. spaghetti, broken into 2-inch pieces and cooked just 5 minutes
1/4 lb. EACH grated sharp Cheddar and Parmesan cheese

90

Heat oil to medium temperature in large skillet. Saute beef, onion and garlic in oil until brown. Add tomato sauce, wine, seasonings and sugar. Cook, covered, over low heat for 30 minutes. Combine sauce with spaghetti noodles and half of both cheeses. Mix well. Mixture should be a little loose. Add a little water if mixture seems too dry. Place in a 2-1/2-quart buttered casserole and top with remaining cheeses. Bake, covered, for 20 minutes at 350°F. Uncover, bake 10 minutes more. Serves 8.

Quick Spaghetti Sauce

This sauce compares favorably with many that take hours to prepare. If you like mushrooms in your sauce, add 1 cup sliced mushrooms to garlic and meat as they saute.

2 tbs. olive oil
2 cloves garlic, minced
2 lbs. ground beef chuck
1 envelope (1-1/2 ozs.) onion soup mix
1-1/2 cup water
3/4 cup dry red wine
1 can tomato paste

1 can tomato sauce
1-1/2 tsp. sugar
salt and pepper
1/2 tsp. EACH basil, oregano
grated Parmesan-Romano cheese
    combination (optional)

Heat oil to medium temperature in large skillet. Saute garlic and ground beef in oil, for 5 minutes. Add remaining ingredients, except cheese and simmer 30 minutes. Serve over spaghetti. Top with cheese, if desired. Serves 8.

Tex-Mex Goulash

This is an unbelievable dish. It can be expanded to feed an army. The proportions can be changed; ingredients can be omitted or doubled. Anything you do just seems to improve it.

1/4 cup vegetable oil
1 cup finely chopped onion
2 cloves garlic, minced
1 lb. very lean ground beef
   (round, if possible)
salt and pepper
1/2 tsp. oregano
1 can (8 ozs.) tomato sauce
2 tbs. wine vinegar
2 tbs. (OR to taste) chili powder

1 can (1 lb.) kidney beans, drained
1 package (1 lb.) corn chips,
   coarsely crushed
1/2 lb. shredded sharp Cheddar cheese
2 cups shredded lettuce
4 green onions, sliced
3/4 cup sour cream
1 can (4.2 ozs.) sliced black olives, drained
tomato slices, cucumber slices,
   alfalfa sprouts, for garnish (optional)

Heat oil to medium temperature in large skillet. Saute onion, garlic and beef in oil. Add seasonings, tomato sauce, vinegar and chili powder. Cover and simmer 10 minutes. Add kidney beans. Lightly butter a 13 x 9 x 2-inch baking dish. Cover bottom with half

92

of the crushed corn chips. Sprinkle with half of the shredded cheese. Spoon on meat-bean sauce. Cover with remaining chips. Top with rest of cheese. The dish can be prepared a day ahead up to this point and refrigerated. Bake at 350°F. uncovered about 15 minutes, or until heated through. Mix lettuce with green onion and spoon on hot casserole. Top with sour cream and olives. Garnish as desired. Serves 6.

1 jar (6 ozs.) marinated artichoke hearts
1/2 cup chopped onion
2 eggs, separated
1 cup soft breadcrumbs
1/3 cup milk
salt and pepper
1/2 tsp. oregano
1/2 tsp. dried mint
1-1/2 lbs. lean ground beef
1/3 cup all-purpose flour
1-1/2 cups water
3 beef bouillon cubes
3 tbs. fresh lemon juice
6 lemon slices

94

Drain artichokes and reserve marinade. In a large skillet, warm 1 tablespoon reserved marinade over medium heat. Saute onion in marinade. In a large bowl, beat egg whites lightly with fork. Add onions, crumbs, milk, salt, pepper, oregano, mint and ground beef. Mix well. Shape into 18 meatballs. Roll each meatball in flour. In a large skillet, over medium heat, saute meatballs in the remaining artichoke marinade. Remove meatballs as they brown. Add water and bouillon cubes to skillet. Mash bouillon cubes into water. Stir until smooth and thick. Stir in lemon juice and lemon slices. Return meatballs to pan. Cover and cook over low heat about 10 minutes. Add artichoke hearts. Cook 1 more minute. Remove meatballs to serving platter. Beat egg yolks slightly. Stir in 1 tablespoon of hot sauce into the yolks (not the other way around), then combine with remaining sauce. Serve over meatballs. Serves 6.

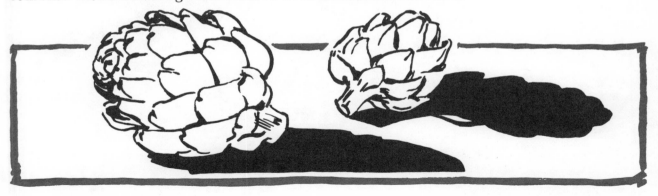

Beef Sukiyaki

2 lbs. beef sirloin
1 cup very thin slices Bermuda
   (OR other sweet) onion
3 stalks celery, cut on angle
   into 1-inch pieces
12 scallions, cut in 1-inch bias pieces
1/2 lb. mushrooms, sliced
1 can (8-1/2 ozs.) water chestnuts,
   drained and sliced

1/4 cup soy sauce
3/4 cup beef bouillon
1/4 cup dry vermouth
1 tsp. sugar
salt and pepper
1 tsp. MSG (optional)
3/4 lb. torn spinach, washed and dried

97

The meat will be much easier to cut if it spends a half hour in the freezer. Use a very sharp knife or a food processor and slice it paper thin (with the slicing blade). Lightly butter a large skillet. Over high heat, quickly brown meat, push to side of pan. Add all other ingredients except spinach. Cook over medium heat, about 5 minutes, stirring often. Add spinach. Cook 2 minutes more. Serve immediately with hot boiled rice. Serves 6.

4 tbs. butter
2 lbs. sirloin of beef cut into 1/2-inch strips
2 cloves garlic
1-1/4 cup dry white wine
1 can beef bouillon (OR chicken bouillon, if making Chicken Stroganoff)
salt and pepper
1/2 tsp. dill
3 tbs. all-purpose flour
1/2 lb. fresh mushrooms, sliced
1/2 cup sliced green onion
1-1/2 cups sour cream (can substitute part thick plain yogurt)
paprika, for garnish (optional)
lemon slices, for garnish (optional)
chopped parsley, for garnish (optional)

98

Melt 2 tablespoons butter in skillet over medium heat. Saute beef and garlic in butter for 5 minutes. Add 1 cup of wine, bouillon, salt, pepper and dill. Cover and simmer about 20 minutes, or until meat is tender. Mix flour with remaining 1/4 cup of wine to form a paste. Stir into meat. Cook until sauce thickens. In another skillet, melt 2 tablespoons butter over medium heat. Saute mushroom and green onions in butter until tender, about 5 minutes. Add to beef mixture. Add sour cream and just heat through. Do not boil. Arrange on serving platter and garnish with paprika, lemon slices and chopped parsley, if desired. Serves 6.

Hint: Goes perfectly with hot, buttered broad noodles and chutney. For an interesting change, substitute cubes of chicken breast for beef.

Marinated Flank Steak

This recipe will *make* your reputation as a good cook. The meat must marinate several hours, at least, to tenderize properly, so a little forethought is necessary.

Try marinating chicken and fish in this mixture too. If refrigerated, this marinade will keep for up to three weeks.

1 tsp. ground ginger
1 tsp. dry mustard
1 tbs. molasses
1/2 cup soy sauce

1/4 cup vegetable oil
3 cloves garlic, minced
2 small flank steaks, 1 lb. each

100

Mix together all ingredients except meat. Place in plastic bag with flank steaks. Secure closed. Marinate 3 to 4 hours at room temperature, turning a few times, or in refrigerator up to 8 hours, turning occasionally. Remove meat from marinade. Broil for 5 to 7 minutes, depending on thickness of steak, turn and broil another 5 minutes. The steak should be served rare. Slice on angle. Serves 6.

Hint: Leftovers make superb sandwiches.

This is another one of those indestructible leftover dishes. Almost anything you have in the refrigerator can go into it. It improves with each addition.

1/4 cup vegetable oil
1/2 lb. sliced mushrooms
2 stalks celery, sliced on angle
1/2 cup chopped onion
1/2 cup chopped green pepper
1 clove garlic, crushed
4 tbs. soy sauce
2 tbs. dry sherry

salt and pepper
2 cups cooked rice
2 cups leftover roast beef
  (or pork or chicken) cut into strips
2 peeled, seeded and diced
  fresh tomatoes (optional)
3 eggs
3 cups shredded lettuce

101

Heat oil in large skillet to medium-high temperature. Saute vegetables in oil 3 to 4 minutes. Mix soy sauce, sherry, salt and pepper with rice. Add to vegetables along with meat. Add tomatoes if desired. Heat through, stirring occasionally. Do not overcook. Just before serving, slightly beat eggs; add to mixture. Cook about 3 minutes. Add shredded lettuce, mix lightly, serve at once so lettuce stays crisp. Serves 6.

Veal Madeira

1-1/2 lbs. veal scallops
1-1/2 cups all-purpose flour seasoned with salt and pepper
1 tsp. tarragon
1/4 cup butter
1/4 cup Madeira (or to taste)

102   Try to get the butcher to pound the veal. If you are doing it yourself, pound them between 2 pieces of waxed paper to 1/4-inch thickness. Place seasoned flour and tarragon in plastic bag. Put veal in and shake to coat. Shake off excess. In a large skillet over high heat, melt butter. When bubbly, add veal and cook quickly until brown on both sides, about 5 minutes total. Remove to warm serving platter. Pour Madeira into pan and lower the heat. With a fork, scrape all brown bits adhering to bottom into sauce. When heated through, pour over meat and serve immediately. Serves 6.

Veal with Artichokes

2 jars (6 ozs. each) marinated artichoke hearts, drained (reserve marinade)
1 tbs. butter
2 cloves garlic, minced
2 lbs. veal round in 1/2-inch strips
flour seasoned with salt and pepper
1/2 tsp. EACH tarragon and dill
1 can (1 lb.) solid pack Italian tomatoes (good quality counts here)
1/2 tsp. sugar
1/2 cup dry white wine or dry sherry

Combine 2 tablespoons of the artichoke marinade and butter in a large skillet. Place over medium heat. Saute minced garlic in butter-marinade mixture for 2 minutes. Dust veal strips with seasoned flour. Sprinkle with tarragon and dill. Add to skillet. Brown veal strips. Add tomatoes, sugar and wine. Simmer until tender, about 10 minutes. Add drained artichokes. Simmer a few more minutes. Serves 6. Serve with French bread.

103

VEGETARIAN MAIN DISHES

No doubt about it, vegetables have poor press. They need a dynamic public relations person to change their image from food that you tolerate because it is good for you to food that is delicious, that you look forward to enjoying. The first thing to do is change some of the names of the vegetables. Words like eggplant, squash, turnips and carrots, conjur up the wrong image. Winter acorns sound better than squash, shallots are more interesting than onions, and anything sounds better than lima beans.

The trouble with vegetables starts in early childhood. Parents who never made their peace with vegetables somehow transmit that feeling to their children, who soon decide that these foods with the strange names are not for them.

Within the last few years things have begun to look up for vegetables. Now that we know a vegetarian dish can be every bit as delicious as a meat dish, we are duty bound not to pass along our prejudices to the next generation.

If you are trying to introduce a reluctant diner to the pleasures of a vegetable entree, try Lasagna Swirls, page 106 or Linguine with Vegetables, page 116. They might be surprised! Ten million vegetarians can't be wrong.

If you have a favorite spaghetti sauce of your own, substitute it for the can of tomato sauce and omit the seasonings.

2 tbs. olive oil
2 cloves garlic, minced
1 cup chopped onion
1/2 lb. mushrooms (optional)
1 can (15 ozs.) tomato sauce
salt and pepper
1 tsp. EACH basil, oregano and sugar
12 lasagna noodles
2 packages (12 ozs. each) frozen chopped spinach, defrosted and squeezed dry
1 cup grated Parmesan-Romano cheese combination
1-1/2 cups Ricotta cheese (cottage cheese will do, but is not as flavorful)
dash nutmeg
Parmesan-Romano cheeses, to sprinkle on top

Heat oil to medium temperature in skillet. Add garlic and onions. Saute until limp.

Add mushrooms and saute 5 minutes more. Add tomato sauce, salt, pepper, sugar, basil and oregano. Simmer about 10 minutes. Cook lasagne noodles, no more than 8 minutes. They should not be completely tender. Rinse thoroughly with warm water. Sprinkle with a few drops of olive oil to prevent sticking. Mix together spinach, cheeses, and remaining seasonings. Mixture should be stiff. Spread about 1/4 cup of cheese mixture lengthwise on each noodle. Roll up and stand on end (*not* seam side down) on a buttered 10-inch round, 2-1/2-inch deep casserole dish. Pour sauce over noodles.* Bake covered 30 minutes at 350ºF. (60 minutes if cold). Sprinkle with additional Parmesan-Romano cheeses. Serves 6.

*Dish may be prepared ahead to this point and refrigerated for up to 2 days in advance.

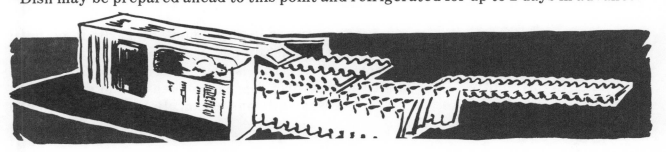

Broccoli-Rice Casserole

The brown rice gives this dish a distinctive flavor. If you think you don't like brown rice, try it, you might be surprised!

2 tbs. vegetable oil
1 cup chopped onion
2 cloves garlic, minced
1 tsp. dill
salt
1/2 tsp. EACH thyme and oregano
1/4 cup chopped parsley
1/2 lb. mushrooms, sliced

1/2 cup chopped green pepper
2 lbs. broccoli, cut into small florets
   with stem portion sliced thin
1/2 cup cashews
3 cups cooked brown rice
1 cup shredded Gruyere cheese
1/4 cup grated Parmesan cheese
1 cup sour cream (can substitute part yogurt)

In large skillet heat oil to medium temperature. Saute onion and garlic in oil until limp. Add dill, salt, thyme, oregano, parsley, mushrooms, green pepper and broccoli. Cook over medium heat, stirring often until broccoli is just tender, about 7 minutes. Add nuts. Lightly butter a 9 x 13-inch baking dish. Spread cooked rice in dish. Cover with vegetable-nut mixture. Top with cheeses and sour cream. Bake at 350°F. for 20 minutes, or until bubbly. Serves 6.

These simple ingredients combine to provide a very satisfying meal. If you don't have Mozzarella cheese, Swiss works just as well. You can change the proportions, or add other vegetables in the refrigerator that need eating.

2 lbs. potatoes, boiled in their
   jackets and slightly undercooked
1/2 cup melted butter
salt and pepper
1-1/2 lb. ripe tomatoes, sliced
1-1/2 tsp. basil

1-1/2 cups grated Mozzarella cheese
8 hard-cooked eggs, coarsely chopped
1/2 cup fresh chopped parsley
3 tbs. fresh chopped dill
   (or 1 tsp. dried)
1/2 cup grated Parmesan cheese

109

Peel cooked potatoes and cut them crosswise into 1/4-inch thick slices. Pour 2 tablespoons of the melted butter over the bottom of a large shallow casserole. Arrange potato slices on bottom of buttered casserole, in one layer. Salt and pepper them. Arrange tomato slices on top of the potatoes. Sprinkle with salt, pepper and basil. Sprinkle grated Mozzarella on top of tomatoes. Combine eggs with rest of melted butter, parsley, dill and more salt and pepper. Spread egg mixture over cheese. Sprinkle dish with grated Parmesan and bake 20 minutes at 350°F. Serves 6.

6 ozs. medium-wide egg noodles
1 tbs. EACH butter and vegetable oil
1/2 cup chopped onion
1 large clove garlic, minced
1/2 can (1 lb.), Italian tomatoes, undrained
1/2 small can tomato paste
1 tsp. sugar
1/2 tsp. basil

salt and pepper
2 eggs
6 ozs. cottage cheese
1 cup grated sharp Cheddar cheese
1 package (12 ozs.) frozen chopped
  spinach, defrosted and squeezed dry
1/2 tsp. dried sage (optional)
1/4 cup grated Cheddar cheese

110

Cook noodles "al dente," no more than 5 minutes. Toss with butter to prevent sticking. Heat oil to medium temperature in a large skillet. Saute onion and garlic in oil until limp. Add tomatoes, tomato paste, sugar, basil, salt and pepper. Simmer 15 to 20 minutes, stirring occasionally. In a bowl, beat eggs. Add cheeses, spinach, more salt and pepper, and sage. In 13 x 9 x 2-inch baking dish, spoon a few tablespoons of tomato sauce on bottom. Place 1/2 of the cooked noodles on top, then 1/2 of the egg-cheese mixture, 1/2 of the tomato sauce. Repeat, ending with tomato sauce. Cover and bake at 400°F. for 25 minutes. Uncover, sprinkle with a little more Cheddar cheese and bake 5 more minutes. Serves 4.

4 eggs, separated
6 medium potatoes, cooked in jackets until fork tender, peeled and finely chopped
1-1/2 cups creamed cottage cheese
1 pkg. (10 ozs.) frozen chopped spinach, defrosted and squeezed dry
1/2 cup chopped onion
salt, pepper and nutmeg
1/2 cup grated Parmesan cheese

111

    Slightly beat egg yolks. Combine with potatoes and remaining ingredients, except egg whites. Stir together until well mixed. In a separate bowl, beat egg whites until they form stiff peaks. Fold them into the potato mixture. Turn mixture into a buttered 2-quart casserole. Bake at 375°F. for 45 minutes, or until firm. Serves 6 to 8.

Baked Vegetable Melange

2 tbs. vegetable oil
1-1/2 cups zucchini, sliced about
   1/2-inch thick
1-1/2 cups diced green pepper
1-1/2 cups thinly sliced
   or shredded carrots
1/2 cup chopped green onion
   (use some of the green portion)
2 small cloves garlic, minced
1/2 tsp. EACH basil and oregano

salt and pepper
1 cup sour cream
   (yogurt can be substituted for all or part)
1/2 cup grated Parmesan-Romano
   cheese combination
3 tbs. chopped parsley
1/2 tsp. thyme
1/4 cup Parmesan-Romano cheese
1/4 cup breadcrumbs

112

Heat oil to medium temperature in large skillet. Saute vegetables in oil for 3 minutes. If there seems to be a lot of liquid, pour off some. Mixture should not be soupy. Stir in basil, oregano, salt and pepper. Mix together remaining ingredients except 1/4 cup Parmesan-Romano cheese and breadcrumbs. Stir into vegetables. Spoon into buttered casserole. Sprinkle with last 2 ingredients. Bake at 350°F. for 20 to 30 minutes. Do not overcook. Serves 6.

Vegetable Stroganoff

This is a wonderful sauce that can be made with any vegetable. You can use one vegetable, two or any combination. It's a good way to get rid of the bits and pieces that accumulate in the refrigerator.

3 tbs. butter
1/2 lb. chopped mushrooms
1 cup chopped onion
salt and pepper
1 tsp. EACH tarragon and dill
1 tbs. soy sauce
3 tbs. dry red wine
2 cups sour cream AND 1 cup thick plain yogurt
   (can change proportions of sour cream to yogurt)
6 cups of raw vegetables, use one or more:
   choose from broccoli florets, cauliflower florets, carrots, zucchini and cabbage
3/4 lb. egg noodles, cooked al dente
1/4 lb. cup minced scallions

114

Melt butter in skillet over medium heat for 5 minutes. Add salt, pepper, tarragon, dill, soy sauce and wine. Simmer about 5 minutes. Stir in sour cream and yogurt and heat just until warm. Do not boil. Keep warm over *low* heat. Steam coarsely chopped vegetables till just tender, about 7 minutes. Butter prepared noodles. On a large platter, assemble the Stroganoff: spread cooked noodles on bottom, followed by steamed vegetables, topped with sauce. If there doesn't seem to be enough sauce, you may add more cream and yogurt. Top with minced scallions. Serves 6 to 8.

1/2 cup Ricotta cheese (cottage cheese will do)
1/4 cup Parmesan-Romano cheese combination
1/2 head cauliflower, cut into florets
1/2 bunch broccoli, cut into florets
2 tbs. EACH olive oil and butter
2 cloves garlic, minced
1/2 cup chopped onion
1/2 lb. mushrooms, sliced
1 tsp. salt
1/4 tsp. pepper
1/4 tsp. crushed red pepper (optional)
1/2 tsp. dill
1/2 lb. linguine noodles
grated Parmesan-Romano cheese

116

Combine Ricotta and 1/4 cup Parmesan-Romano cheese. Set aside in a warm place. Steam or undercook cauliflower and broccoli florets (less than 5 minutes). In a large skillet heat butter and olive oil to medium temperature. Saute garlic and onions for a few minutes. Add mushrooms, salt, pepper, red pepper and dill. Saute another 2 minutes. Stir in cauliflower and broccoli and continue cooking over medium heat, stirring to coat the vegetables with oil. If the mixture becomes too dry, add a little water. Cook vegetables about 5 minutes; they should not be overcooked. Cook linguine "al dente," about 5 minutes. Drain well, toss with a little olive oil to prevent sticking. Pile linguine on large serving platter. Spread cheese mixture on top. Top with vegetable mixture. Sprinkle more grated cheese on top. Serves 6.

1-1/2 cups raw bulgur wheat
2 tbs. butter
1 tbs. vegetable oil
1-1/2 cups chopped onion
2 cups sliced fresh mushrooms
2 cups minced green peppers
2 tbs. soy sauce

2 tbs. sherry
1/2 tsp. marjoram
salt and pepper
1-1/2 cups cottage cheese
3/4 cup crumbled Feta cheese
4 eggs, slightly beaten
paprika

118

Soak the bulgur wheat in 1-1/2 cups boiling water for 20 minutes. Drain. (This step cannot be omitted or bulgur wheat will not absorb the liquid in the casserole.) Melt butter in skillet over medium heat. Add oil. Saute onion, mushrooms and peppers until just tender. Remove from heat. Add soy sauce, sherry, marjoram, salt and pepper to vegetables. Spread bulgur evenly on the bottom. Cover with vegetables. Place mixed cheeses on top of vegetables. Pour beaten eggs with a little salt and pepper over everything. Sprinkle with paprika. Bake uncovered 45 minutes at 350°F. Let stand a few minutes before serving. Serves 6.

1/4 cup vegetable oil
2 green peppers, finely chopped
3 medium onions, chopped
1/2 lb. mushrooms, sliced
3 cups cooked rice (see page 146)
1 cup milk
1 cup grated Parmesan cheese (can substitute part Cheddar)
1 cup chopped fresh parsley
2 eggs, well beaten

119

Place oil in saucepan over medium heat. Lightly saute peppers, onions and mushrooms for 3 minutes. Add rice. Stir together remaining ingredients, adding eggs last. Lightly pile mixture into a buttered baking dish. Place dish in a pan of hot water. Bake at 325°F. for 1 hour, or until set. Serves 6 to 8.

An excellent sauce for spaghetti or any other pasta. Serve with salad for a complete meal.

120

1 tbs. EACH olive oil and butter
1/2 cup chopped onion
2 cloves garlic, crushed
2 cups cubed eggplant
1-1/2 cups sliced mushrooms
1/2 cup chopped green pepper
1/2 cup Burgundy wine

1/2 small can tomato paste
1/2 can (1 lb.) Italian tomatoes, undrained
salt and pepper
1 tsp. EACH basil and oregano
2 tbs. fresh chopped parsley
1/4 cup Parmesan-Romano cheese combination

Heat oil and butter in a large skillet to medium temperature. Saute onion and garlic until limp. Add eggplant, mushrooms and green pepper. Saute 5 minutes. Add wine and remaining ingredients except parsley and cheese. Mix well. Cover and simmer over low heat for 20 minutes, stirring occasionally. Just before serving, mix in parsley and Parmesan-Romano cheeses. Serve over pasta with additional cheese. Serves 4.

Mushroom Almond Chop Suey

3 tbs. vegetable oil
salt and pepper
2 cups thinly sliced onion
2 cloves garlic, chopped
3 cups diagonally sliced celery
2 green peppers, seeded and cut into strips
1 lb. fresh mushrooms, sliced
1 cup chicken broth

2 tbs. cornstarch
1/4 cup soy sauce
2 cups mung beans
1 can (7 ozs.) water chesnuts, drained
   and sliced (optional)
1/2 cup slivered almonds, lightly toasted

121

   Heat oil with salt and pepper in saucepan over medium heat. Saute onion, garlic, celery and green pepper in oil for 3 minutes. Add mushrooms and saute another 3 minutes. Add chicken broth. Cover and simmer about 5 minutes, or until vegetables are done but still firm. Mix together cornstarch, water and soy sauce. Add to vegetables and stir until thick and glossy. Add mung beans, water chestnuts, if desired, and almonds. Stir just until reheated; vegetables should still be crisp. Serves 6 to 8.

BRUNCHES

Brunches have come of age. For many it is the perfect meal. It happens in the mid-morning, before the insults of the day have accumulated, when people are usually perky and hungry and ready to have a good time.

Screwdrivers, Bloody Marys, and Champagne Punch are great eye-openers for the drinking crowd. Wonderful soups (hot or cold), eggs fixed a million different ways, quiches, fish, cheese, salads, homemade breads are all brunch fare; it is the meal of unlimited possibilities. One thing to remember about brunch is to prepare it ahead so you don't wind up center-stage preparing two eggs at a time while hungry people sit, watch and wait.

When the food and the ambience are just right a brunch can last all day. If you have not yet gotten the brunch habit, hurry. You are missing a great dining experience.

The changes you can make in this recipe are limited only by your imagination.

2 tbs. butter

1-1/2 to 2 cups assorted vegetables: onion, green pepper, celery, scallions, zucchini, cooked potato (use as many as you like)

about 1/4 cup cooked crumbled bacon; bits of ham, smoked sausages, cooked sausages, dried beef or leftover roast beef may also be used

5 eggs

1/4 cup dry chablis OR dry sherry

salt and pepper

1-1/2 tsp. herbs: choose 2 or 3 from chervil, tarragon, basil, thyme, dill, chives or parsley

1/2 cup shredded Cheddar OR Swiss cheese

4 to 5 tomato slices

alfalfa sprouts, for garnish (optional)

Melt butter in large, oven-safe skillet over medium heat. Saute vegetables in butter until they are limp. Combine meat (if no meat is desired, omit that step), eggs, wine, salt, pepper, herbs and 3/4 cup cheese. Reserve remaining cheese for topping. Pour over vegetables. The larger the surface of the pan, the less time it will take to bake. Bake 15 minutes in 350°F. oven. Add tomato slices and reserved cheese. Bake 10 to 15 minutes longer, or until eggs are done. Sprinkle with alfalfa sprouts. Let set 5 minutes before cutting. If using a round baking dish, cut into wedge-shaped pieces. Serves 4 with leftovers.

Bagel and Lox Pie

This adaptation of the traditional duo makes a superb brunch or lunch dish. A fresh fruit compote is a nice accompaniment. Shredded ham may be substituted for the lox.

5 onion bagels
1/3 cup melted butter
1/2 tsp. dill
3 tbs. melted butter
1 cup finely chopped onion
8 eggs, lightly beaten

2-1/2 cups milk
salt and pepper
1 tbs. EACH fresh chopped parsley and chives
6 ozs. shredded lox (use the salty variety)
　OR shredded ham
1 cup shredded Swiss cheese (Jarlsberg, if possible)

126

Cut bagels into small pieces. Dry in 250°F.oven for 20 minutes. Using a food processor or blender, convert small pieces into crumbs. This can be done a day ahead. Mix crumbs with 1/3 cup melted butter and dill. Press into bottom and sides of 10-inch quiche pan or 13 x 9 x 2-inch baking dish. Bake 8 minutes at 400°F. until brown. Cool on wire rack while preparing rest of dish. Melt butter in small skillet. Saute onion about 2 minutes. Combine onion with remaining ingredients except cheese. Sprinkle cheese on prepared crust. Pour egg mixture over cheese. Bake at 350°F. for 30 minutes or until puffed and done. Let stand 5 minutes before cutting. Serves 6 to 8.

Self-Sauce Souffle

2 cups fresh (or frozen) peas
3/4 cup chicken broth
2 tbs. cornstarch
1/2 cup light cream
salt, pepper and dill
2 hard-cooked eggs, sliced
8 raw eggs
1/3 cup milk
1/2 tsp. Dijon mustard
3/4 cup EACH shredded Swiss and Cheddar cheese

Combine peas and broth in saucepan over medium heat. Cook until peas are just tender. Do not drain. Combine cornstarch and cream. Add to peas along with seasonings. Cook until thick and bubbly. In a 10-inch glass pie pan, arrange sliced hard-boiled eggs. Add peas. In a blender or food processor, combine raw eggs and milk. Add remaining ingredients and process or blend until smooth. Pour carefully over egg-pea mixture. Bake at 375°F. for 40 minutes, or until puffy. Cut into wedges and serve. Serves 6 to 8.

Bulls-Eye Eggs

This is the easiest brunch to prepare. The whole thing can be assembled in 15 minutes. Use a large flat baking dish. A large pizza pan works fine.

2 cups shredded Swiss cheese
10 eggs
1/2 cup sour cream
1/2 cup plain thick yogurt
3 tbs. dry sherry (optional)

salt and pepper
1/2 tsp. dill
1 tbs. fresh chopped chives
paprika (optional)

128

Butter a 2-quart baking dish. Sprinkle 1 cup of Swiss cheese on bottom. Carefully break eggs over cheese, take care not to break yolks. Mix together sour cream, yogurt, sherry and seasonings, except paprika. Spread over eggs. Bake for 10 minutes at 325ºF. Sprinkle with remaing Swiss cheese. Bake another 5 to 10 minutes or just until eggs are set. Dust with paprika. Serves 6 to 8.

Substitute 3 cups of croutons (packaged ones are fine) for the English muffins for a delicious variation.

6 English muffins, split and toasted
1-1/2 cups shredded Swiss cheese
8 eggs, lightly beaten
3 cups milk
1 tsp. prepared mustard

1/2 tsp. onion powder
salt and pepper
1 tsp. dill
1 tbs. fresh chopped chives
1/4 lb. cooked bacon, drained and crumbled

129

Butter a large shallow baking dish (a cookie pan with sides works fine). Place muffins in pan in a single layer; you can cut the muffins to make them fit the dish. Sprinkle cheese over muffins. Combine remaining ingredients, except bacon and pour over muffins. Bake for 15 minutes at 325°F. or until eggs are set. Top with crumbled bacon. Bake 5 minutes more. Serves 6 to 8.

The crust makes this dish most unusual and it doesn't get soggy! It is also delicious prepared a day ahead and reheated.

1-1/4 cups finely crushed saltines,
   OR other crackers (about 30)
1/3 cup melted butter
1/2 lb. bacon, cooked, drained and crumbled
   (reserve 2 tbs. bacon drippings)
1 cup chopped onion
1/2 lb. Swiss cheese, shredded
   (Jarlsberg, if possible)

1 cup sour cream OR plain thick yogurt
8 eggs, slightly beaten
salt and pepper
1/2 tsp. dill
1/2 cup shredded Cheddar cheese

Combine crumbs and melted butter. Press onto bottom and sides of a 10-inch quiche dish. Sprinkle cooked bacon over crust. In a small skillet, saute onion in 2 tbs. of bacon fat until limp. Combine sauteed onion with rest of ingredients, except cheese. Pour into shell. Bake for 30 minutes at 375°F. or until knife inserted into center comes out clean. Sprinkle with Cheddar. Bake 2 to 3 minutes more. Let stand 10 minutes before serving. Serves 6 to 8.

This recipe can be expanded to feed a large crowd. It can be prepared a day ahead or at the last minute. There is nothing to burn or undercook.

3 cups day old bread cubes
  (any kind of bread)
1/4 cup butter
1/4 lb. grated Swiss cheese
  (Jarlsberg, if possible)
3 cloves garlic, crushed
salt and pepper
1 tsp. sweet Hungarian paprika
1 cup sour cream

1-1/2 cups plain yogurt
4 scallions, minced
salt and pepper
dash paprika
10 hard-cooked eggs, sliced
1/2 lb. bacon, cooked, drained
  and crumbled
1-1/2 cups grated Cheddar cheese
alfalfa sprouts, for garnish (optional)

Mix together bread cubes, butter, cheese, garlic, salt, pepper and 1 teaspoon paprika. Place on a cookie sheet. Bake at 400°F. for 10 minutes, or until bread is toasted and cheese is melted. Cool. Transfer mixture to food processor or blender in batches. Process or blend until well combined. In a bowl, combine sour cream, yogurt, scallions, salt, pepper, paprika and dill. Thin with a little milk if mixture appears too thick. Pat

crumb mixture into a 13 x 9 x 2-inch baking dish. Arrange sliced eggs over crust. Sprinkle with crumbled bacon. Top with sour cream-yogurt mixture. Sprinkle with grated Cheddar. Bake about 15 minutes at 400°F. until everything is heated through and cheese is melted. Just before serving, sprinkle with alfalfa sprouts, if desired. Serves 8 with leftovers.

This can be varied to suit whatever is left over in the refrigerator. Bacon can be used in place of the ham. Monterey Jack cheese can replace the Cheddar and 1 cup fresh sliced mushrooms can be added when sauteeing the onions.

2 tbs. butter
1/2 cup sliced green onion (include some green tops)
10 eggs
1-1/2 cups milk
salt and pepper
1 cup cooked shredded ham
2 cups grated Cheddar cheese

134

Melt butter in skillet over medium heat. Saute onions in butter until limp. In a bowl, beat eggs with milk and seasonings. Add sauteed onions, ham, and 1-1/2 cups cheese. Pour into a buttered 2-1/2 quart baking dish or casserole. Bake 30 minutes at 350°F., or until mixture is set. Sprinkle with remaining cheese. Bake until cheese is melted. Serves 6 to 8.

Spinach Tarte

This is a very simple version of a quiche. There is no crust to make. It can be served hot or cold and it travels well.

2 tbs. butter
3/4 cup chopped onion
3/4 cup thinly sliced mushrooms
1 package (12 ozs.) chopped spinach, defrosted and squeezed dry
4 eggs, lightly beaten
3/4 cup grated sharp Cheddar cheese
1/2 tsp. Worcestershire sauce
salt and pepper
dash nutmeg

135

Melt butter in skillet over medium heat. Saute onion and mushrooms in butter, about 5 minutes. Combine all ingredients. Place in buttered 13 x 9 x 2-inch dish or 10-inch quiche pan. Bake 45 minutes at 350°F. or until eggs are set. Serves 4.

This is a brunch or a supper dish. Leftovers can be eaten cold.

3 tbs. butter
1/2 cup minced onion
1-1/2 cups diced cold cooked potatoes
10 eggs
3/4 cup half-and-half

salt and pepper
3 tbs. fresh minced parsley
1 tbs. butter
4 tomatoes, quartered

136

Melt 3 tablespoons butter in large skillet over medium heat. Saute onions and potatoes until lightly brown, about 7 minutes. With a fork, beat together eggs, half-and-half, salt and pepper until blended. Pour over potatoes and onions. Cook over medium-low heat, gently lifting mixture from the bottom as it cooks, until it is set but still moist. Meanwhile, lightly sprinkle tomatoes with salt and pepper. Melt remaining 1 tablespoon of butter in a small skillet. Saute tomatoes in butter for just a few minutes. Tomaotes should still be firm. Place eggs on serving platter. Arrange tomatoes around eggs. Serves 6 to 8.

Artichoke Heart Frittata

2 pkgs. (10 ozs. each) frozen artichoke hearts, thawed
3 tbs. butter
salt, pepper and dill
6 slices bacon, cooked, drained and crumbled
12 eggs
3/4 cup grated Parmesan cheese

Rinse artichoke hearts in boiling water. Dry. Melt butter over medium heat in a *137* skillet. Saute artichokes until lightly browned. Place in heavily buttered shallow baking dish. Season. Sprinkle with crumbled bacon. Beat eggs with whisk and stir in cheese. Pour over artichokes. Bake in upper part of oven at 400°F. for 10 minutes, or until just set. Serves 6 to 8.

Upside Down Quiche

The crust on this quiche forms as it bakes. It is delicious hot or cold and travels well.

1/2 lb. cooked bacon, crumbled
1-1/2 cups shredded Swiss cheese (use Jarlsberg, if possible)
1/2 cup finely chopped onion OR scallions
1 can (12 ozs.) whole kernel corn, drained (optional)
3 cups milk
1-1/2 cups biscuit mix
8 eggs
salt and pepper
1/2 tsp. dill

138

Combine bacon, cheese, onion and corn. Spread on bottom of buttered 10-inch quiche pan. Combine remaining ingredients in food processor or blender. Process or blend for 30 seconds, or until well combined. Spread on top of bacon mixture. Bake for 35 minutes at 400°F. or until knife comes out clean when inserted. Let stand 10 minutes before serving. Serves 6 to 8.

3 tbs. butter
3 tbs. vegetable OR olive oil
6 small unpeeled zucchini cut in 1/4-inch slices
3 scallions, diced
10 eggs
salt and pepper
1/2 tsp. oregano
1 tbs. EACH fresh chopped parsley and chives
1/3 cup grated Parmesan cheese
1/3 cup grated Swiss cheese

139

Heat butter and oil to medium temperature in large skillet. When bubbly, add zucchini and scallions. Saute a few minutes until limp. Beat together eggs, salt, pepper, oregano, parsley and chives. Add to skillet. Cook over low heat until just set. You can speed the process by cutting through the eggs with a spatula and letting the uncooked egg run underneath. Top with cheeses. Broil for two minutes. Watch carefully. Serves 6 to 8.

MEAL MAKERS

This section provides a grab-bag of "meal makers" and includes a vegetable dish that doubles as a relish, a fruit curry that goes with everything, a bread that can be made with just 3 ingredients. It is a small part of my collection of treasures gathered over the past 25 years, and is one of the most useful sections of this cookbook.

The great mushroom controversy is: To Wash or Not To Wash. The solution is simple. If the mushrooms seem dirty, wash. If they are snow white, no need to wash. If you do wash them, don't let them soak in water or they will absorb it and then render the water when they cook; perhaps spoiling the dish.

142

1/4 cup butter
1 cup minced onion
1-1/2 lbs. mushrooms, sliced
2 tbs. all-purpose flour
1/3 cup water

2 tbs. dry sherry OR Madeira wine
salt and pepper
1/4 cup chopped parsley
1/2 cup sour cream
chopped parsley, for garnish (optional)

Melt butter over medium heat in skillet. Saute onion in butter until golden. Add mushrooms. Saute five minutes. Add flour, water and wine. Stir mixture until smooth. Add salt, pepper and parsley. Cook about 5 minutes. Add sour cream and heat through. Do not boil. Garnish with a little parsley. Serve hot. Serves 6.

This combines perfectly with any sweet-sour dish, and can be used as a sidedish in place of "plain old noodles." It is a special treat.

1 pkg. (10 ozs.) very fine egg noodles
3 eggs, lightly beaten
salt and pepper
1 tbs. fresh chopped chives
dill (optional)

143

Slightly undercook noodles in boiling salted water. They should still resist slightly when bitten. Drain thoroughly. Mix well with remaining ingredients. Put tablespoonfuls of noodle mixture on hot buttered griddle or skillet. Cook over moderate heat until bottoms are golden brown. Turn with a spatula and brown the other side. Serve immediately. Serves 6.

This is a wonderful accompaniment to Chicken Piccata, page 76, or other poultry dishes. It is perfect with stroganoff too.

10 ozs. medium-wide egg noodles (homemade if possible)
1/4 cup butter (not margarine)
1/3 cup slivered blanched almonds
1 tbs. poppy seeds
1 tsp. paprika
1 tbs. fresh chopped parsley
salt and pepper

144

Slightly undercook noodles in boiling salted water. They should still resist slightly when bitten. In a small skillet, melt butter over medium heat. Add almonds. Cook until golden. Add butter, almonds and remaining ingredients to drained noodles. Add a little more butter if mixture seems dry. Serve immediately. Serves 6.

Noodles Florentine

This recipe combines starch and vegetable in one dish. It's a perfect choice when you don't have time to make both.

1 pkg. (8 ozs.) medium-wide egg noodles, cooked and drained
1/4 cup melted butter
salt and pepper
1 cup grated Swiss cheese
2 packages (12 ozs. each) frozen chopped spinach, drained and squeezed dry

1 cup sour cream (can substitute part yogurt)
1 tsp. dried tarragon
1 tbs. fresh lemon juice
1/4 cup grated Parmesan cheese
2 tbs. breadcrumbs

145

Combine all ingredigents except Parmesan and breadcrumbs. Place in buttered 2-quart casserole or baking dish. Bake at 350ºF. for 15 minutes. Add Parmesan and breadcrumbs. Bake until lightly browned, about 10 minutes. Serves 6 to 8.

This is the only recipe I ever use to cook rice. No matter what any recipe says, if it calls for cooked rice, I cook it my way. No need to buy the fancy, packaged varieties of rice. There is no agreement on whether it is better to wash rice by rubbing between the fingers or not. If I have time, I wash, if not, I let it go. I can't tell the difference. It is, however, a little less caloric if some of the starch is washed off.

1-1/2 cups raw white rice (washed or not)
146   1-3/4 cups cold water
1/2 tsp. salt
1 tbs. butter or margarine

Put everything is a medium saucepan (that has a tight-fitting lid). Bring to a rolling boil, uncovered. Give it a quick stir, put the lid on, *then* turn down the heat as low as possible. If you can't get the heat low enough, place saucepan on an asbestos pad (with the heat on). Steam for 20 minutes without removing the lid. Turn off heat for 5 minutes, leaving saucepan on burner. Fluff with a fork. It's ready. Serves 6.

In this recipe, a simple vegetable is transformed into something very special. The recipe was the secret of a fine restaurant until . . .

2 pounds carrots, scraped and cut into 1/4-inch thick slices
1-1/2 cups diced celery; include some of the leaves
1/2 cup chopped onion
3/4 cup dry white wine
1/4 cup sugar
1/4 cup butter
1 tsp. dill
salt and pepper

In a large suacepan mix everything together. Cook, covered, over low heat, until carrots are just tender. Do not overcook. Serves 6 to 8.

147

Make twice as much as you think you'll need. It still won't be enough. It goes perfectly with many poultry and pork dishes, and is a natural with Thanksgiving turkey.

Some people like to chop up the fruit a bit. I prefer to leave it whole. Proportions of fruit are not important. You may add or omit fruits, as desired.

1 can (1 lb., 13 ozs.) peach slices
1 can (1 lb., 17 ozs.) apricot halves
1 can (1 lb.) pear halves
1 can (1 lb., 4 ozs.) pineapple chunks
3/4 cup firmly packed brown sugar
3 to 4 tsp. curry powder
1/3 cup melted butter

149

DRAIN FRUIT THOROUGHLY ON PAPER TOWELS (very important). Place fruit in 2-1/2-quart casserole. Mix rest of ingredients and pour over fruit. Bake uncovered for 45 minutes at 350°F., turning gently once or twice.

Use either rice or barley, or a combination. Serve cold or at room temperature.

3 cups steamed rice OR barley (should be dry so it can take up the moisture
   of the dressing)
3 tbs. fresh lemon juice
1 tsp. EACH salt and pepper
1/2 cup olive oil
1 cup peeled, seeded and diced cucumber
3/4 cup EACH thinly sliced radishes and parsley
1/3 cup EACH minced green pepper and sliced scallions (with some green tops)
1 tbs. EACH dill and fresh chopped chives
salt and pepper
tomato wedges for garnish (optional)

150

Keep rice warm. In food processor or blender combine lemon juice and salt. Add olive oil in a stream until it is well combined. Toss immediately with warm rice. Add rest of ingredients. Chill for at least an hour. Garnish with tomato wedges if desired. Serves 6 with leftovers.

Zucchini Bake

This goes well with any kind of meat or fish. It is an adaptation of zucchini pancakes (and tastes almost the same), but takes much less time to prepare.

3 cups coarsely grated zucchini (use food processor)
3 eggs
1/2 cup minced green onion (use some green tops)
2 small cloves garlic, minced
1/2 cup grated Parmesan cheese (can use part Romano)
1/2 cup (more or less) biscuit mix
1 tsp. EACH dill and fresh chopped chives
salt and pepper
2 tbs. vegetable oil
1/4 cup grated Parmesan cheese

151

Press as much moisture as possible out of zucchini. Combine remaining ingredients. It should have a thick batter-like consistency. If it seems too stiff, add another egg. Place in an oiled 9 x 13-inch baking pan. Bake 30 minutes at 350°F. until brown. Top with additional Parmesan cheese, if desired. Serves 6.

Sweet-Sour Eggplant

Eggplant lovers love this; non-eggplant lovers admit that it is delicious. It combines wonderfully with mid-eastern dishes or with roast meats. It also can be used as a relish. It is a very special antipasto offering.

152

2 lbs. eggplant, cut in slices about
   2 inches across and 1/4-inch thick
olive oil
salt and pepper
1/2 cup wine vinegar
3 tbs. olive oil

1 tbs. honey
1 tbs. fresh chopped parsley
1 tbs. fresh OR 1 tsp. dried basil
1 tsp. fresh OR 1/2 tsp. dried mint
1 tsp. sugar

Place eggplant on a non-aluminum pan (important). Enamel or glass is fine. Brush with olive oil and broil until eggplant is soft and lightly browned on both sides. Remove eggplant pieces as they brown. Season with salt and pepper. Keep warm. In a bowl, blend remaining ingredients. Marinate eggplant until ready to use, an hour or a day. Can be stored in refrigerator for up to 3 days. Serve at room temperature. Serves 8.

20 min.

Eggplant Everything

 30 min.

If you prepare just one eggplant dish, this should be it. It is a relish, a vegetable; can be served hot or cold, freezes well, improves with age and is easy to prepare. The recipe can easily be doubled or tripled.

3 tbs. vegetable oil
2 cloves minced garlic
1 cup finely chopped onion
2 cups peeled eggplant, in small cubes
1 small jar (2 ozs.) chopped pimento
2 tbs. fresh lemon juice

2 heaping tbs. catsup
1 tsp. salt
1/2 tsp. pepper
1/2 tsp. paprika
2 tsp. prepared horseradish
1 tsp. sugar

Heat oil to medium temperature in large skillet. Saute garlic and onion in oil until golden. Add eggplant and pimento and saute a few more minutes. Mix remaining ingredients together in a bowl. Stir well. Pour over vegetables. Cook, covered, over low heat, stirring gently, until eggplant is tender but not mushy, about 20 minutes. Serves 6.

Beer Bread

For an instant bread, this is surprisingly good.

3 cups biscuit mix
2 tbs. sugar
1 bottle (11 ozs.) beer, at room temperature
1/2 cup shredded Cheddar cheese (optional)

154   Combine all ingredients until just blended. Pour into a buttered loaf pan. Bake 45 minutes to 1 hour at 350°F., or until toothpick inserted into center comes out clean.

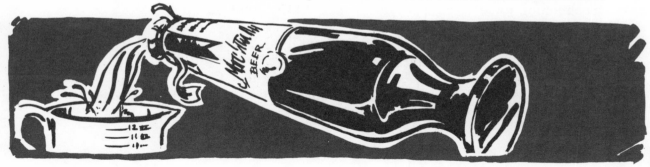

Curried Pineapple

An exceptionally good side dish for a Chinese dinner.

1/4 cup butter (not margarine)
1 fresh pineapple, peeled and cut into bite-sized chunks
1/2 tsp. salt
1 to 2 tbs. curry powder
1/4 cup firmly packed brown sugar
4 green onion, chopped

In a medium saucepan, melt butter over high heat. Quickly stir in pineapple chunks. Add rest of ingredients and stir until heated through, about 3 minutes. Serve hot. Serves 6.

DESSERTS

Sometimes a lovely dinner seems to run out of steam toward the end and comes to a halt with a scoop of ice cream or a store-bought cake for dessert. If the dinner could speak, it would probably say, "Please, let's not end this way!"

A good dinner deserves a just dessert (oow!), a so-so dinner needs a good dessert, and sometimes even a poor dinner can be redeemed by a smashing dessert. That's a lot to ask of a banana or a bunch of grapes, but *Fast & Delicious* desserts can do it.

Strawberry Pie

If you enjoy summer fruit, this is the pie to make again and again. You can substitute blueberries, peaches or nectarines for the strawberries.

1-1/4 cups crushed graham crackers
2 tbs. sugar
3 tbs. melted butter or margarine
1 heaping quart strawberries

1 cup sugar (use a little less
 if the fruit is very sweet)
3 tbs. cornstarch (use a little more
 if the fruit is very ripe)
2 tbs. fresh lemon juice

Make graham cracker crust by mixing together first 3 ingredients in a 9-inch pie plate. Press crumbs firmly onto bottom and sides of pie plate. Bake at 350°F. for 8 minutes. Cool. Meanwhile place half of the berries and remaining ingredients in a large saucepan. Cook over medium heat, stirring, until mixture becomes thick and glossy. Let it cool or the filling won't jell properly. (Very important! It took me years to figure this out.) When the cooked mixture stops smoking, add rest of the berries. Stir gently to coat. Pour into crust and chill. Good advice: if more than 6 people are having dessert, make two pies.

Cream Cheese Cupcakes

These look so spectacular that you feel a little guilty that they're so simple. Double or triple it for a large group.

paper cupcake liners
3/4 cup graham cracker crumbs
2 tbs. melted butter
1 tsp. sugar
1 pkg. (8 ozs.) cream cheese, softened

1 tsp. vanilla
1/4 cup sugar
1 egg
1 can (1 lb., 4 ozs.) prepared canned pie fillings: cherry, blueberry or pineapple

159

Place cupcake liners in muffin tins. In mixing bowl, combine crumbs, butter and sugar. Place 1/2 teaspoon of mixture in each liner. Pat down. Place remaining ingredients, except topping, in mixing bowl or food processor. Mix or process until well blended. Should be very smooth. Pour on top of crumbs, filling about half full. Bake 8 to 10 minutes at 375°F., or until lightly browned. When cool, top with different kinds of prepared pie fillings. Make 18 small cupcakes.

Actually, this is neither a pie nor a cake, just a delicious light dessert.

6 tbs. butter, softened
1 cup sugar
3 eggs, separated
1/3 cup EACH all-purpose flour, lemon juice

1 tbs. grated lemon rind
1/2 tsp. salt
1-1/2 cups milk

160   In mixing bowl, cream together butter and sugar. Beat in egg yolks, one at a time, beating well after each addition. Beat in flour, lemon juice, lemon rind and salt. Pour milk in slowly, beating constantly. Wash beaters. In another bowl, beat egg whites with a pinch of salt, until they hold stiff peaks. Stir one fourth of the whites into the lemon mixture (not the other way around). Then fold in the remaining egg whites. Pour the mixture into a well buttered 1-1/2-quart souffle dish and set the dish in a baking pan. Add enough boiling water to the baking pan (not the souffle dish) to reach one third of the way up the sides of the souffle dish. Bake for 1 hour at 350°F., or until top is golden. Serve warm. Serves 6.

Quick Chocolate Cake

This is even faster and better than a cake mix.

1 cup sugar	2 tsp. vanilla
1-1/2 cups all-purpose flour	1/2 cup oil
1/3 cup cocoa	1 cup cold water
1 tsp. baking soda	2 tbs. white vinegar
1/2 tsp. salt	powdered sugar (optional)

Preheat oven to 375°F. Stir together sugar, flour, cocoa, baking soda and salt in an 8-inch square pan. Make 3 "wells" and add oil, water and vinegar to each. Stir quickly and thoroughly. Place *immediately* (important) in oven. Bake 20 to 25 minutes or until center is puffed and the sides begin to pull away. Cool. Sprinkle top with powdered sugar, if desired.

Cocoa Fudge Casserole Cake

This cake can be a last minute decision.

1 cup all-purpose flour	1 tsp. vanilla
2 tsp. baking powder	2 tbs. melted butter
1 tsp. salt	1/2 cup chopped walnuts
2/3 cup sugar	3/4 cup firmly packed brown sugar
2 tbs. cocoa	1/4 cup cocoa
1/2 cup milk	1-1/4 cups boiling water

162

Sift flour, baking powder, salt, sugar and cocoa together 3 times. Combine milk, vanilla and butter in a measuring cup. Add to dry ingredients. Stir until just moistened. Add nuts. Stir to combine. Spread in buttered 6-cup casserole. Combine brown sugar and cocoa. Sprinkle over top of batter. Pour boiling water over entire cake. Bake 50 minutes at 350°F. Serve warm with vanilla or peppermint ice cream, or whipped cream.

Upside-Down Rhubarb Cake

1 tbs. butter
3 cups diced rhubarb
1-1/4 cups sugar
2 tbs. all-purpose flour
1 tsp. orange rind
1/2 tsp. cinnamon
1 cup all-purpose flour

2 tbs. sugar
2 tsp. baking powder
1/2 tsp. salt
1 egg
3 tbs. heavy cream
1/4 cup frozen orange juice,
  undliuted and thawed

Butter an 8-inch square baking pan with the 1 tablespoon of butter. Sprinkle rhubarb into pan. Combine next four ingredients. Sprinkle over rhubarb. Make batter by combining 1 cup of flour with remaining ingredients, except orange juice. If mixture seems too thick, add a little more cream. Spoon over rhubarb mixture. Bake at 350°F. for 25 minutes. Spread top with orange juice. Bake 15 minutes longer. Invert hot cake into a cake plate. Serve with whipped cream, if desired.

If you have bananas on hand, you have the main ingredient for this spectacular dessert.

1/3 cup butter (not margarine)
1/4 cup firmly packed dark brown sugar
6 to 8 bananas cut once lengthwise and then in half
2 tbs. fresh lemon juice
1/2 tsp. cinnamon
1/4 cup banana liqueur (if possible) OR Grand Marnier
1/2 cup rum
vanilla ice cream to serve 6

Melt butter in a skillet over medium heat. Add sugar. When bubbly, add bananas. Add lemon juice, cinnamon and liqueur. Cook about 5 minutes, stirring constantly. Bananas should not be mushy. Warm rum in saucepan over low heat. Pour over bananas and ignite immediately. When flame dies, serve over ice cream. Serves 6 to 8.

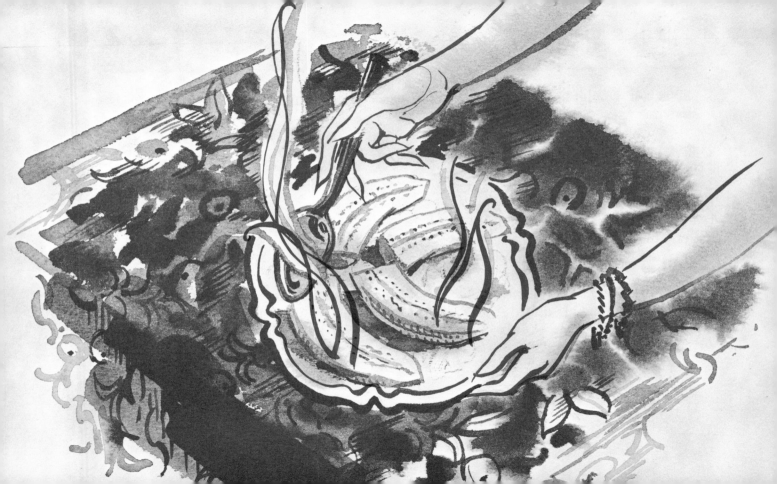

Streusseled Blueberries

This is a wonderful summer dessert. It can be made only when fresh blueberries are in season.

6 cups fresh blueberries
3 tbs. fresh lemon juice
2/3 cup firmly packed brown sugar
1/2 cup all-purpose flour
1/4 tsp. EACH salt and nutmeg
1/4 cup butter
sweetened whipped cream (optional)

166

Mix blueberries with lemon juice. Pour into buttered 9-inch square baking dish. Mix sugar with flour, salt and nutmeg. Cut in butter coarsely. Rub between fingers until well blended. Sprinkle evenly over berries. Bake for 20 minutes at 375°F. Serve warm with whipped cream, if desired. Serves 6 to 8.

Grapes with Honey Cream

For some reason this looks spectacular. Everyone expects it to taste delicious and it does. Lovely sherbet glasses help the presentation

1 cup sour cream
1/3 cup honey
3 tbs. Drambuie OR an orange flavored liqueur
3 tsp. lemon juice
1-1/2 lbs. seedless grapes, washed and dried
coarse raw sugar for garnish (optional)

Mix together everything but grapes and coarse raw sugar. Just before serving, toss the grapes with the sauce and spoon the mixture into sherbet glasses. Top with raw sugar, if desired. Serves 6.

Plum Cobbler

1 can (1 lb., 14 ozs.) purple plums
1/4 cup orange juice
2 tbs. sugar
2 tbs. cornstarch
1/2 tsp. cinnamon
1-1/2 cups biscuit mix
1/2 cup milk
2 tbs. melted butter
2 tbs. firmly packed brown sugar.

168

Drain and pit plums. Reserve syrup. Place plums in a 1-1/2-quart baking dish. Combine syrup, organge juice, sugar, cornstarch and cinnamon in saucepan. Cook over medium heat until thick and glossy. Boil 1 minute. Pour over plums. Place in 400°F. to bake while making topping. Mix together biscuit mix and milk. Drop onto bubbling plum mixture. Drizzle melted butter and brown sugar over dough mixture. Bake 20 minutes, or until top is golden. Serve warm with ice cream. Serves 6.

There must be literally hundreds of brownie recipes, but not many that can be mixed in a saucepan. You won't even have a bowl to wash.

2 squares unsweetened chocolate
1/3 cup butter or margarine
2 eggs, lightly beaten
1 cup sugar
1/2 tsp. salt
1 tsp. vanilla
3/4 cup all-purpose flour
1 cup (or less) coarsely chopped walnuts

In a large saucepan, melt chocolate and butter together over medium heat. Cool. Add eggs. Stir in sugar, salt and vanilla. Mix with a spoon. Add flour and walnuts. Mix again for a minute. Pour into a buttered 8 or 9-inch square pan. Bake 30 minutes in a 350°F. oven. Brownies should be soft. Cool in pan. Cut into squares.

Even if you think you have the ultimate chocolate mousse recipe, try this. It's made in food processor or blender. It can be doubled or tripled and is the perfect dessert for so many meals.

1/4 cup very cold milk
1 envelope unflavored gelatin
3/4 cup boiling milk
170 6 tbs. dark rum OR Grand Marnier
1 egg
1/4 cup sugar
1 tsp. vanilla
pinch salt
1 pkg. (6 ozs.) semi-sweet chocolate chips
1 cup heavy cream
2 ice cubes

Place cold milk in food processor or blender. Add gelatin. Process or blend to soften about 30 seconds. Add boiling milk. Blend another 30 seconds to a minute to dissolve gelatin. Add remaining ingredients, except cream and ice cubes. Blend or process until smooth. Add cream and ice cubes. Blend until cubes melt. Pour into bowl or parfait glasses. Chill. Serve with whipped cream, if desired.

If you are doubling or tripling, do it in batches. Most processors don't take large quantities of liquid.

Timesaver: If you're running late, place in freezer for 1/2 hour to speed chilling.

This is a bonus recipe. When offered with other confections, they disappear first. They keep well, mail well, and are just plain delicious. They are not, however, for the dieter.

1-1/2 cups walnut halves
1 cup blanched whole almonds
1/2 tsp. salt
172 1/2 cup butter
3 egg whites, stiffly beaten
1 cup sugar
3/4 cup all-purpose flour

Place nuts and salt in 13 x 9-inch baking dish. Put in a 325°F. oven for about 15 minutes, or until nuts are toasted. Remove nuts from pan and set aside. Melt butter in pan. Fold together stiffly beaten egg whites, sugar and flour. Fold in toasted nuts. Spread in pan with melted butter. Bake 30 to 35 minutes at 325°F., stirring occasionally to break apart large clumps of nuts. Bake until brown.

Apple Nut Cake

No peeling, no slicing and no sifting for this cake. It takes just a few minutes to prepare if a food processor is used to grate the apples.

1 tbs. fresh lemon juice
unpeeled apples grated to make 2 cups (packed)
1 cup sugar
1/4 cup vegetable oil
1/2 cup coarsely chopped nuts
1 egg, beaten
1 tsp. vanilla

1 cup all-purpose four (unsifted)
1 tsp. baking soda
1 tsp. cinnamon
1/2 tsp. nutmeg
1/4 tsp. cloves
1/4 tsp. salt

173

Sprinkle lemon juice over grated apples. Combine apples and sugar. Mix thoroughly. Add next 4 ingredients and beat with a spoon. Add dry ingredients. Beat to combine. Place in buttered and floured 8 x 8-inch baking dish. Bake 40 minutes at 350°F. or until toothpick inserted into center comes out clean. Cool 10 minutes in pan. Invert onto rack and finish cooling. Serve with vanilla ice cream.

Butterscotch Squares

This is a delicious and easy dessert. Not many guess the mystery ingredient— zucchini. The recipe can easily be doubled.

1/3 cup butter or margarine	1 tsp. baking powder
1 tbs. hot water	1/8 tsp. baking soda
1 cup firmly packed brown sugar	1/2 tsp. salt
1 egg	3/4 cup peeled, diced zucchini
1 tsp. vanilla	1/2 cup chopped walnuts
1 cup all-purpose flour (unsifted)	1/3 cup butterscotch chips

174

In saucepan over medium heat, melt margarine with hot water. Place in a mixing bowl. Add sugar and beat well with a fork. Cool. Add egg and vanilla; beat again. In a separate bowl, mix dry ingredients together. Add to sugar mixture. Stir until just blended. Stir in zucchini and nuts. Pour mixture into a buttered and floured 9 x 9-inch pan. Sprinkle with butterscotch chips. Bake for 25 minutes at 350°F.. Cool in pan. Cut into squares. Serves 6.

3/4 cup water
1/2 cup sugar
1/2 cup orange juice
1/4 cup fresh lemon juice
2 tbs. slivered orange peel
1/2 cup sweet sherry
6 firm Bartlett pears, cored and quartered (not peeled)
1/4 cup slivered toasted almonds (optional)

175

    Combine water, sugar, orange juice, lemon juice and orange peel in saucepan over medium heat. Simmer for 4 minutes. Add sherry and pears. Cook about 10 minutes. Pears should be cooked but still firm. Remove from heat. Add almonds, if desired. Chill. Serve with heavy cream.

This pie quickly becomes a family favorite. It is a birthday pie, a Christmas pie and a company pie. There are infinite variations, but somehow the basic pie seems to endure. A 10-inch pie should serve 8 or 10 people, but it doesn't: everyone finds room for another small piece. It's a tradition in our house that the guest of honor, or the birthday person gets to scrape the pan.

176

1/2 of a 1 lb. package butterscotch-nut icebox cookie dough (found in a rolled package
    in the dairy section of the supermarket);
    dough can be varied; try chocolate chip
1-1/2 quarts vanilla (or any other) ice cream
6 tbs. canned chocolate or fudge sauce
4 egg whites
pinch of salt
6 tbs. granulated sugar

Be sure the cookie dough is very cold. Cut it into very thin slices with a sharp knife. Place on the bottom and sides of a 10-inch pie plate. Don't worry about holes in the crust or improperly cut slices. They will disappear while baking. Bake at 400°F. for 6 to 8 minutes, or until lightly browned. Refrigerate or freeze until well chilled. Soften ice cream just a bit. Place evenly in chilled crust. Top evenly with 4 tablespoons of the chocolate sauce. It can be frozen at this point, to be completed just before serving. When ready to serve, set oven at 500ºF. In a small bowl, beat egg whites with salt until soft peak stage. Gradually add sugar and beat till they hold stiff peaks. Cover ice cream evenly with meringue, making sure meringue touches crust at all points. Drizzle 2 tablespoons of chocolate sauce on top, swirling with a spatula to give a marbled effect. Bake 2 to 3 minutes at 500ºF., until lightly browned on top. Serve immediately, or freeze and serve up to 3 days later. If freezing and serving later, place in refrigerator an hour before serving. It is a little better to serve it right away rather than freeze, but no one will know the difference.

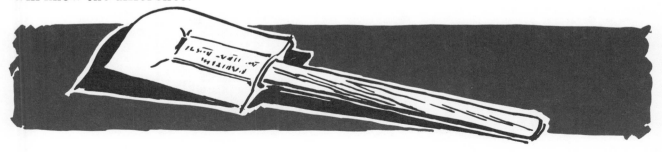

INDEX

179

180